Passage
to
America

Passage to America

AMERICAN MELTING POT

Gopi Krishena

PASSAGE TO AMERICA
AMERICAN MELTING POT

iUniverse books may be ordered through booksellers or by contacting:

iUniverse
1663 Liberty Drive
Bloomington, IN 47403
www.iuniverse.com
1-800-Authors (1-800-288-4677)

ISBN: 978-1-5320-6739-6 (sc)
ISBN: 978-1-5320-6740-2 (e)

Library of Congress Control Number: 2019900976

Print information available on the last page.

iUniverse rev. date: 01/25/2019

Preface

Please note that this is a story of an immigrant to USA and his family growing in USA. This pertains to real lives and living peoples. To keep and maintain privacy of all characters in story the actual names have been changed. The book describes a real story of a real family currently living in USA. The story is about an average family living in USA which immigrated in 1971 to USA. It touches the immigration policy of America to stick with under laws and without any exploitation of any one race and religion and faith. This is meant to unification of all races, cultures and to produce a real and unique MELTING POT and on the principle that world is becoming COMPACT and small and the only country is UP on that is the country which we call the GREAT UNITED STATES OF AMERICA. The most immigrants come to this country (USA) simply seeking freedom, human dignity, human rights and simply human survival. The most immigrants are looking for social, economic and religious freedom. The story describes the motivational circumstances of a family.

Sam!

This is Nana and want to tell you the story of your life and how you ended up the way you are and what caused it. Believe me it was not your fault. It was just an unfortunate accident of nature or almighty whatever you may believe in. I do have a firm belief that God loves you immensely as He is the one who saved you and there is a purpose decided by all mighty to accomplish through you for our family and for rest of the world we are connected with.

But there is no way I can tell you your story and what happened to you unless I tell you my story and the story of our family first. Ryan got excited and anxious to listen all this.

I want to tell you the story of our family as I either heard or lived. I know you can hear, understand and analyze everything in your mind. Although I know you cannot speak yet your facial expressions and smiles explain a lot to me. Do you want to hear 'MY STORY'? Sam smiles indicating his acceptance.

My great grandfather Roy moved from western state of Maharashtra in India to Panjab state in northern India in early 1800. He belonged to Mahratta's/Pesewa who ruled western states of India before British rule in India. Matamatas were very dedicated to love for their motherland as demonstrated by Shivaji Mara Hatta in Indian history. I never knew and was never told by any of the ancestors the motivation of his migration to Panjab during British Rule of India. I am guessing probably looking for a job or looking for land to cultivate. He settled in Ambala district of Panjab state in a small village of Panchkula. This small village fell into one of the backward and remote areas of then Panjab state of India. This village had no water or electricity. Only water source was a well in the village. The water was drawn by buckets and carried to houses in pitchers on head by men and women. This area is currently known as the modern city of Chandigarh and is part of union territories of India. This area has developed now to modern way of life. I still wonder what made my great grandfather migrate. Perhaps in those days without any modern means of transportation the people could move. How they moved I wonder. May be by bullocks, horses or by foot as compared to most recent migrations of humans happening in modern times. The railroad and buses did not exist. Walking three to four miles to any modes of transportation was usual and very common.

I do not know how many sons and daughters he (Roy) had. I was told one of his son was Nate Ram Godse who married Druga Devi. Sam, Nate Ram and Durga Devi were my great grandparents. Sam, this may not mean anything to you as your problems are bigger than listening to a story. From your face and smile I can tell that you do want me to tell you my story to you. I know you are interested in knowing about how you came into existence. Of course you are the God Given Gift to our family and we all love you. I saw a smile on Sam's face.

I heard Nate Ram died in an early age and my great grandmother Durga known in the family as a nick name 'JEE' left to bring up two children. One boy named Paru and one girl named Ganga. Paru and Ganga were in their teen years when their father died. Paru Dass was my grandfather and Ganga Devi was my grand auntie. Jee was a very strong woman as per my father's words who gave me a picture of her before I left India. He even told me an incident which happened in her life. One time she was travelling and she took a bus. The bus was almost full. A man was sitting in lady side seat and she was standing next to him. She requested him for the seat as per prevailing courtesy ethics and rules in those days in British India. The man did not move and did not give up his seat for her. She instantly slapped the man in front of peoples. He got so ashamed that he left his seat for her. As I see her picture she sure appears to be a woman with self-respect and confidence. In Indian culture men are supposed to leave their seat for women, olds and children. This is not always a Must Do but a courtesy culture thing.

Durga (Jee) was going through rough times when her husband passed away and she had two children (A boy and a girl) to grow. She had no income source and had no support. She decided to move away to a remote place called village of Ramgarh. Ramgarh was a very small rural town about twenty miles away from today's modern Chandigarh sitting just in the foot of the Himalayas. In the North of this village are the high peaks of mountains of Himalayas and to the east is a huge River called GHAGER flowing out of the high mountains to the agricultural fields of Panjab. The real irony of the area was that every time monsoon rains come, the river Gagger will over flood making transportation tough through buses. Only reliable source of transportation was railway trains. Finally a new city of Chandigarh was planned by a French Architect. A dam was constructed on Ghaghara River to construct a manmade Suk Hana Lake in city of newly planned city of Chandigarh. Although the city has not developed yet the area start turning from real backward and remote to a modern planned city.

This is a time when my grandfather Peru Doss and my grand auntie Ganga Devi were grown up. Ganga Devi was the elder sister of my grandpa. She got married and moved to a city named Patiala in Panjab which was about fifty to sixty miles from Chandigarh area. Patiala is also as Patiala District of Panjab. She and her husband owned several real estate properties in that town of including three houses which still exist in that town but have been rebuilt and street have been rebuilt also.

My grandfather Peru Doss married and stayed in Ramghar. He had three sons and four daughters which means I had two uncles and four aunties, Sam! This is like you have uncle Surej and auntie Dipika on your mom side. Of course you also have uncle and aunties on your dad side.

The oldest son of my grandfather (Peru) was Braham Dev who was my father and was born in November 1906. Now you can understand that he was your great grandfather or great grand Nanna. He grew up around Mubarak Purr which is in Ambala district 0f newly formed state of Haryana or old Himachal Pradesh. This was considered those days as remote and backward area of then state of Panjab and Haryana. The highest school grade available in the area school system was 8th grade. Therefore my father had to move from this rural are to a city Patiala in district Patiala of Panjab. My grand auntie Ganga Devi lived there and my father moved to live with her. My dad made this move all to continue his education further to high school as well as to college. And where he completed his high school and college in Patiala city. After his school years he got married to my mom whose name was Lakshmi Devi.

My mom's maiden name was 'Manbhari' which mean in our language the person who will fulfill your heart desire. She always fulfilled mine and I am the living proof of that. Without her and her dedication my existence would not have ever happen. She never went to any school but her intelligence was imp parallel. She learned limited reading and writing at home. This tells people always wanted to learn more and more if given a chance and opportunity. Just to prove herself and her dedication to family she changed her name to Lakshmi Devi which meant in our language the goddess who teaches us the art of being content and feeling fulfilled all the time in spite of our ever changing circumstances and ups and downs of life. She was not only a selfless woman but very great like any other selfless mother living today and as all mothers are always selfless and would take care of their children even if inconvenient for them and they never expect anything in return from their children. All they do for their children is nothing but selfless.

My great grand auntie (Buaa) never had any child of her own. After her husband died, she asked my father and uncle to live in Patiala. She gave my father and uncle separate homes to live. She had three homes when my great grand uncle died who had a unique hobby to fly and keep Pigeons. She kept one for herself and gave other two to my father and uncle to live with their respective families.

My father took a job with Panjab Police after finishing his two years of college education. Most of the police employees were only middle school pass but my father had an Associate Degree from college, which enabled him quick promotions in Police department during British Rule and he was promoted to a rank of Police Inspector. He maintained his position in British India and later on in free India. Even two years of college education was very scarce in India. He was a very honest person and will conduct his police duties in a very fair and legal manner. Unfortunately the department as a whole was nothing but a cell of corruption and bravery. Even today I never hear anything positive about the department. The rich and the powerful use police in their favor by bribing them and the weak and the poor only suffer.

My father always took his job very seriously and his job took him to different places on a very short notice. He kept the family either in Patiala or in Ramgarh with his parents so that children could go to school on a regular basis. My grandfather also owned mango gardens and some agriculture land in a small village of Panchkula village. Currently this area is in the area of modern city of Chandigarh. He sold mangoes and other agriculture produce like wheat and corn for his living. He also worked for a Sirdar who was like a small prince governing a small district to collect revenue from other land owners. He kept a horse to go around and a buffalo for his milk and butter. Even I got a chance to ride a few time with my grand pa when he went around to different agricultural farms. It was always a few hours ride extending half to full day.

This was somewhere in 1930's. My father's first born was my oldest sister. She was followed by my four older brothers of mine. Three of my brothers and my oldest sister were born in 1930's probably (just guessing) 1932, 1934, 1936, and 1938 and one older brother Kapil was born in 1940 and my youngest sister was born in 1946.This is all my guess as I was told by my mother all of you guys are two years apart and all of you had approximately two years difference in their year of birth. My oldest sister was Shila and I had four older brothers and one younger sister. Our family mostly stayed in Patiala. Sometime my father will take all the family to the city of his job posting for a few months in a year. His job required him to move frequently in then Panjab state of India. If his stay at certain location of his job was very brief depending on crime area he would leave the family in our home town of Patiala where his auntie lived or in village of Ramgarh where his parents lived. He would visit us all every 2 to 3 weeks as permissible by his job situation.

The year was 1942 and the struggle of India's independence was getting more and more intense. This is what I heard from my father and mother when I was still growing. I do not know at what age. My mother, my older sister and my older brothers were all visiting my grandfather's home in Ramgarh in old state of Panjab in Ambala district. The month I was told was September and the sun sign in case you believe in astrological signs was Libra. This was all documented in my grandfather's handbook along with the date. There was no other way for me to remember or knowing. One thing I do remember as I was growing up that on every birthday my mom (whom I love and miss dearly) would make me to take some food items to temple on our street. That was the way the family celebrated birthdays. I do not know whether that was Hindu culture or something with in the family.

I do not remember much about first three or four years of my life. Only thing I remember that everybody was saying an independence war is going on. I was told that this fight was to liberate India from British Rule. Although I could not understand what is going on but I was perplexed and could figure out that war is something bad whenever and wherever it happens. This kind of talk and what I heard was not the favorite part of my memory or so called history. I was five year old when India's fight for freedom from British rule was almost concluding. Although I was just a child at that time yet I remember processions of masses chanting with slogans of freedom at the same time I witnessed my mother extinguishing normal wood fire in her cooking Chula (A small man made brick oven or earth furnace which was fired by only wood). There were no rules or norms to protect children to stay away from such displays and activities. Finally on August 15, 1947 India became free as I read later in my school days.

But when I look back after travelling through several countries around the world, I see and feel as though India has become free from foreign rulers and became self-ruled and a democratic country yet it lacks in Social and economic freedom for which certain social reform through their own leadership. It is great India has moved towards freedom of press very positively. It has to move more towards human rights, solving social issues in a country of diverse religious existence, which can be achieved by today's leadership and role models of that country's society such as heroes and successful actors of film industry which people follow.

Unfortunately, not any major improvement is happening in some of the basic needs of the society which helps the poor and the disadvantaged due to caste and economic in justice by the people who have it all either by corrupt practices or over bearing government practices or too rich capitalists who have not cared for the welfare of poor workers who actually have served them. The real culture is almost disappearing and the people are divided in between East and West values. Neither of the values are wrong or better but the society has to move towards where the modern humanity has reached scientifically as well towards international culture of acceptance and understanding each other of values.

These were just some fake memories of mine around 1947 in India. The riots of partition started due to division of India into two countries. Panjab state was a border state where we lived. There were riots and unrest all over. Every time there will be a noise of processions or riots or killing my mother would tell us to stay inside the house. She would shut the doors with fear and extinguish any fire and lights in the house. Everything going on around me was beyond my understanding and was simply nothing but confusion. I would get scared and fearful.

Finally came the time for me when my fifth birthday came and I did the same thing which my mom told me to go to temple and give away some food which she gave me. She planted the concept of good 'Karma' in me. This is about the time India became free from British Rule. I have no idea whose policy or rule it was that a five year old has to go to school without knowing what school means and how it will benefit me. I was forcefully admitted to a state run primary school. My aunt always called it a 'Madrasa', an Urdu or Muslim name for a primary school.

Sam, Strange thing with me was, I had no idea why I have to go to school. You are much better than me Sam as you always go to school happily and you know you are going to school to learn new things and make new friends. You always bring good reports from your teachers. My first recollection of my memory of my first day in school that my father while taking me to school stopped at a sweet confectioner shop and took some' Ladoos' which is a famous Indian Sweets. He took enough sweets for all the children in my class so called my class mates. I liked the portion that all my would-be classmates were eating sweets. After that my father was gone. Teacher had taken over the job of teaching the class. Some kids like me had forgotten to do their homework. The teacher got so angry that he beat the little boy like me with his cane. The boy cried and cried so loud but had no effect on teacher. I myself was very scared and perplexed thinking that it might be happening to me. I had no idea whether I was over sensitive or what. I started thinking 'Do I have to learn whatever they have to teach over here in this school or so called Madrasa. Is there a way to bypass whatever they are trying to teach me here? I want to learn new things but cannot stand beating. I started thinking how I can avoid school. I figured out how could avoid coming to school. I had to think and think and plan ahead. Next day my mother and older brother took me to school. After they were gone, I asked my teacher if could go to restroom to pee. The teacher told me 'Yes'. I took that yes to run away and gone from school. This continued for months. I was going to a temple in the middle of down town of the city. I Sat in front of the temple begging and accepting donated food from peoples.

This continued for months. Finally the teacher tried to track me down. He had a good intention In him about me but I could not recognize him as he has already beaten me a few times with his cane. He already gave me popular punishment of holding ears through under legs and sitting on two feet. It was painful physical punishment. The teacher would had me sit right next to him to keep an eye on me. I was desperate to ask him to ask if can go to rest room. Sometime he would let me go and sometimes he would not let me go. All depended on his judgement and mood. I hope India has no teachers like that anymore and such corporal punishment of school kids anymore.

My problem was understanding what they want to teach me and why. My problem was why I should learn how to write and read. Was that a requisite to live for human beings? There was no fun in school those days. No play, no games for me to challenge myself. I could not find any purpose or interest in going to school in my own mind. I had no idea or memory of what I learnt from first two or three years of my school. I had no memory of what I learned in first two or three years of my school, except some bigger kid than me beat me up without any reason. Only thing which was clear to me was that either school teachers or my older brothers or my mother would punish me for running away from school. They all could not figure out that school was just 'Boring". My mother and brothers thought there might me something wrong with school or something I did not like in the school. They took me and transferred me to another school which was just a private school. Unfortunately I could not feel or see a difference. My attitude towards school did not change a bit. Those days if you are admitted in school for the whole year, the school would advance you to next grade if you would pass the final exam. All of a sudden I was admitted into fourth grade and was declared as a number one and extra ordinary student as compared to my other classmates. But in my mind I was still struggling to go to school and still did not like school and would not understand the significance of going to school. I always thought that school was a place to either punish or beat you and not to learn anything fruitful.

India has always boasted about its 5000 years of culture and history and what took them so long to correct such corporal punishment in schools, social justice in society, giving equal rights to woman and protecting the young girls and woman from gang rapes and other inequalities.

SAM, since you are my best friend and have loved me so much but I don't have anybody else to share my pains and suffering. Your nanny was so mad at me today that she took a big knife to kill me and told me to move out. My fault was to take my couple of wine glasses in the evening which I normally take almost every day. This was not new and I am almost addicted to take every day and it helps me overcome some of my allergies and anxiety situations. I have come to home after leaving my job from Cambridge after she fell off stairs in the basement. She almost attacked me with a big knife. I did not say her anything to provoke. Al day she was sleeping on the sofa and watched her Indian movie. It's about ten months she had moved out our bed room and sleeps in a different room complaining about my snoring etc. I do not know for sure what she is complaining about. I thank God to go to sleep and wake up in the morning alive. I have discussed my drinking wine problem with my doctor and he has not objected and said red wine is ok and no hard liquors. May be I have developed alcoholism but I did not hit or killed anyone. I am confused and feel depressed about life some time. I feel I should not have resisted her let her kill me with her knife. She had threatened me like this a few times. But I feel no one asked me whether I wanted my life and if anyone wants my life just take it but do not threaten me. I am not too good with threats of any kind. I usually panic and bring an asthma attack any time somebody threatens me and I feel my life is under someone else control and I am not breathing myself but someone else control my breath and directs me when to take and when not to take. I want to stay free and not everyone telling me what to do and that is the way I grew up being bossed and ruled over most of my childhood by almost everyone I knew. I was never allowed to do whatever I wanted to do. That may a small or big thing. In my life everything was nothing but small things and I was not bothered by any one of them but always wanted to be free in my thinking and in my actions. As I heard later by some of the peoples that you are not a traditional and more or less an individualist. Unfortunately I am still struggling to understand that what and how it relates to my own life. I am simply as God has made me and I have become whatever my circumstances dictated me to continue surviving. I AM STILL TRYING HARD TO FIGURE OUT THE REAL MEANING OF LIFE AND EXITANCE. I AM STILL LOOKING FOR THE QUESTION OF WHO GOD IS. Sometime BHAGWAT GITA guides me and gives me some straight answers.

This was about 1952 and summer vacations were going to begin. My dad decided to take the family to PANCHKULA (small place near Chandigarh in Panjab state in India).This was the place where my grandparents were living. All of my brothers and sisters enjoyed the summer vacations in this village at my grandfather, s house which is close to modern city of Chandigarh. We enjoyed going to mango gardens which he owned and ate different varieties of mangoes. After vacations were over, I was admitted in same high school and my brothers were also in the school which was in Chandigarh. I was in fifth grade. This was first time I started paying attention to school and I started liking my teachers and started paying attention to what teachers were teaching. Most of the classes were held in open and under the shade of a tree outside the school building. I learnt some arithmetic, some Indian languages such as Hindi and Panjabi. I also attended some music classes. In our music class there was only one drum for the whole class. The teacher would give us drum sticks to play on stones. It was fun creating sounds on stones with wooden drum sticks. After having practiced on stones we would get a chance to play on real drum.

After several months my father came and decided to take all of us to his new posting at Kapurthala Panjab India. This place he had been promoted to Inspectors' rank. This city was about hundred miles away from border of current Pakistan. This area was more advanced and urban. I was in fifth grade. My father took me school and left me in fifth grade class after filing my admission papers. I sat through arithmetic and history classes. The third period was of

English language. The teacher was very rude. He asked me to read English. In my previous schools, there was no English unless you were in six grade. I had never learned English language before, the teacher turned me out of the class for not able to read English.

I cried and cried and left school. I was just walking from school. I was trying to figure out my way from school to my home which I thought where my parents were was my home. On the way, I ran into my father who was going to his work.

He asked me why I did not stay in school. First time I said, 'teacher expelled me from class because I did not know English reading and writing'. My father took me back to school. He was dressed in Police Inspector's uniform. He talked to the headmaster of the school and he (My Dad) promised him that he would help me learn the English language at home. I felt protected and taken care. There were only three months left to prepare for the final exam. With my father's help I learned how to read and write English in about two months. In the final exam for fifth grade I made the top of my class in English as well as in other subjects. I started liking school. I started participating in supports. I stopped running truant from school. A few months later again the whole family had to move back to Patiala as my father get transferred to Rampur. After a few months in Patiala, we all joined our father at Rampur. My younger sister was born there. Our family lived in police station. We could see what police does as we could visit all places with in that building. My father was the head in charge for that location. We all named our youngest sister as

'Ghatti' which were her nick name. After a few months later, the schools broke up for summer vacations. My father took us to Panchkula village at my grand pa's place. It was a very hot and humid summer. My youngest sister got sick with malaria there. She died of malaria after a few days. That was my first experience of knowing about death with a diseases about which I learnt later in life. Aru Vedic medicine had no cure for these kind of disease those days. The family believed in Aru Vedic medicine AS ALOPATHIC MEDICINES WERE EXPENSIVE as compared to herbal medicines. She was still less than a year old. Because of her age and a tiny dead body, she was not cremated by rituals. She was buried. It was a sad summer vacation for the family. For me it was just a drained, horrible and confusion causing summer vacations.

At the end of summer vacations, my father took our family to Patiala where our great aunt lived. As all my brothers were in either middle school or high school my father decided to keep us all in State High School Patiala. It was state run government school. I was in sixth grade, brother Mani (Your second elder Nanna) was in 8th grade, older brother Prakash in 10th grade. Older brother Indre and Sushi were already out of school. My oldest brother Sushi went to teachers training and became teacher in state of Haryana. My brother Indre and brother Prakash also took jobs as primary school teachers also. Those days India had a great shortage of teachers as there was shortage of high school pass graduates. Government of India was opening new schools in almost every village and in remote areas of country. Both my elder brothers were recruited in this government plan and started new schools in villages as directed by the government of India at that time. Later on they both took training in teaching.

My oldest sister got married but her marriage failed due to several issues. It was an arranged marriage full of afterwards surprises. My father and my older brothers brought her back home from her in laws in district Ambala. She came home and lived with us and later got herself married. My youngest sister 'Sandy 'was two years behind me in school. She lives in Sangrur Panjab. She has three daughters Bina, Ina and Tina. Bina is married but still lives with my sister. Ina is married and has a baby girl and lives in Patiala, Panjab. Tina is married and has a boy. In India parent's responsibility is never over for their children even if they are married and sometimes parents want to make every decision for them even if they are old enough to make decisions for their life.

My oldest brother Sushi got married to my auntie's younger sister Kamal in Ambala, Haryana. She still lives in Chandigarh, Panjab with her younger son Bintoo my younger nephew in India. My oldest brother Sushi who had died with kidney failure had two daughters and two sons. My older Niece Nira lives in Sunam, Panjab, India and had a son and daughter, who are already grown, married and had probably children. My oldest nephew is Rocky. He and his family lives in Patiala. My youngest niece is Kukrie who lives with her family in a village near Chandigarh in the family she was married to. My own life in USA was so fast and busy which kept me busy and I could not stay in touch with them as often as I wanted to. I could only see them only during my visits to India and unfortunately I did not make too many trips after my parents passed away. I always felt uncomfortable during my trips and became sick every time I visited India. It is A BEAUTIFUL COUNTRY AND MY MOTHERLAND BUT ALS0 IT IS PART OF THE SAME GLOBEL EARTH where all other countries exist and all humans shares the same earth. All humans has nothing except this earth to take care as this earth has been taking care of all life without any complaint. You may simply call it a NATURE or the creation of our GOD.

This was early nineteen fifties. I was about ten year old. I was a lonesome child. I had no friends of my own. My brother had friends of his age. They were all couple of years older than me. I was eating more to keep up with them in every game they played with me. I gained weight and became a little chubby and FAT. Which means in Indian Language just fat and Chubby. My brothers started teasing me with a nick name 'Gopi'. This was after name of a famous comedian in Indian movies those days in Bollywood. His name was Gope. Because I was small they named me Gopi. But I always used to get very angry when anyone would call me Gopi. Even someone say Go...to me I would be furious as I was actually a fat kid. Ryan started laughing. I said you are laughing at me, your nana. Ryan started laughing louder and louder. I could understand what he wanted to say and that is why I love him the most.

Sam made me realize that I had no tolerance to teasing at that time. Every time someone would say me Gopi, I would get so angry and furious that I would start throwing things on them and got into tantrums. One time I threw all my brother's books and note books under our water handle pump and made them wet with water. The more I felt sensitive about teasing, the more every one teased me by saying 'Gopi. I could never control my anger in life.

One evening I came home from school with cough and cold. My mother tried to take care of me, she gave me some tea and told me to go to sleep. I could not go to sleep and coughed all night. Next day she took me to a doctor. He gave me some medicine but nothing happened to me. No relief. I continued coughing. In addition my, breathing got disturbed. I was wheezing and feeling very hard to breath. I could not breathe for days and days. My breathing was disturbed and labored. My mother took me to different doctors who were allopathic and some aryuvedic doctors. Nothing helped me. Only thing I remember were staying awake and gasping for a breath of air. I could not breathe normally, but doctors could not diagnose my problem. Only thing I remember was staying awake for nights and trying to have a normal breath. No medicine was helping me and I was getting worse and worse. I was just struggling for a breath of air and still being in air. My father was away and he was informed about my condition. He could not come but he told my mother to take me to a doctor he knew who was educated in England. Dr. Malaria was a British educated doctor who practiced as a private doctor. My oldest brother took me on his bicycle to the doctor and my mother walked herself to his pharmacy which was almost in the middle of the city called 'Chowk' in Indian language. After examining me, the doctor first time diagnosed me suffering from Asthma the doctor asked my mother if anybody in our family had asthma. She said, "Yes my father had asthma." On the top of this my father mother, grandfather and grandmother were all chain smokers. They all smoked Hookah with a water pipe, their room always looked like on fire and filled with smoke.

I responded very well to the asthma treatment and I felt normal in a very short period of a few days. I was put on a continuous medicine for months. The day I would forget my medicine, I would get sick again at night. I would get up gasping for air during my sleep and would start wheezing. The doctor told me to sleep with a 'Lily capsule' under my pillow and take that capsule as soon as I feel disturbed and labored breathing I was wondering why I could not take even free air from the atmosphere for my wellbeing. Ryan, I am telling you this because you are going through these problems and there is no explanation some times and no answer of Why Me. This is about fifty years ago, Ryan.

Now let us talk about some fun things I did. I and my older brother to whom you call Nana2 did lot of things together. We made kites and flew them. We collected broken glass pieces and ground them and used glue to put on thread we used for kite flying. This was a prevalent support those days we could cut lot of neighbor's kite strings with the flying thread we made with powered glass and glue.

We became so good in kite making, flying and producing the thread for flying that we started selling kites for our pocket money. We enjoyed this way to make money and could collect enough money for our own interests. This was in early nineteen fifties. My dad was sent home on an early retirement. The life in the family changed. His pension was about five dollars a month. All of us in the family started finding firsthand the meaning of 'Poverty'. Our family was common class financially those days. It started sinking to lower class. We were of the highest caste and traditionally not allowed to do anything of the lower caste jobs. All this was made by the traditional nature of the society those days when humans were not treated equal and caste system plagued India

My three older brothers were working on jobs as teachers and were taking care of themselves. My two sisters and we two brothers were still depended on my parents. I still remember some midafternoon my mother would tell us that we did not have anything to cook in the evening. She would go to a neighbor and borrow some flour to make Indian chapattis. She would pay back that flour sometimes later when she would have. That was the real India when neighbor took care of neighbor just fighting hunger. Finally my dad took a secondary job to compensate his government pension which was hardly five dollars of modern times. One evening he brought lot of waste paper home from his office. My older brother and myself took that paper and made envelopes for shopkeepers. The shopkeepers and many other sweat shop owners bought these envelops for packing the goods they sold. My brother and I made money for our pocket allowance and we spent that money on seeing movies.

One evening my brother and his friends were going out. I had no idea what and where they would go. I just followed them and joined in their mission. This was the company of my elder brother and his friends and they were all older than me. I had no idea where they were going and what they would do. They all went to a peach garden which was owned by somebody we never knew. Five of us were plucking peaches and mangoes which was like stealing from that garden. The owners found out and came over us. Everybody ran away but I was still standing there and picking peaches from ground under a tree. The owners caught me. I was alone. Everybody else including my own brother fled away. The owners were some men and some women. The owner lady caught me. She took me to a cottage which was in the center of gardens. I was scared but she was nice to me. She told me to help her in making earthen balls. These balls which were made out of plain soil and were about half inch diameter. These balls they were using to fly away the birds from fruit trees. They used bow and arrow with these balls.

After couple of hours, she freed me. I came home scared and confused. Ryan started laughing that nana was in trouble. I asked Ryan! Are you laughing at Nana's stupid things? Ryan laughed more loudly. That was his way of saying "Yes"

Another time again, I was following my elder brother and his friends. They all went to a huge swimming pool which was just the part of a flowing Canal. While they were all swimming, I was standing and bathing in about my knees deep water in the canal. They (older friends of my brother) lifted me up and threw me in deeper water. I was in deep water and had no practice to swim and had little idea of how to swim. I was drowning and gasping for air to breathe. They finally noticed me drowning and took me out of deep water. I got so scared from deep water that I never learned how to swim. That was the end of my water supports career. I could never get over my fear of how to swim and I could never get over my Asthma.

It was about 1957,I entered high school as a junior and I do not remember much of my years in grade school. I heard teachers were fighting to get me in their class but I had no idea why they all wanted me to BE IN THEIR CLASS. After few days I found out that the school principal had assigned me to Grade A high school class. There were A, B, C, and D grade in high school classes in state High School, Patiala. I studied math, English, science, History and Geography, and medical basic sciences such as hygiene and physiology and Sanskrit as an optional subject. In 1958 I graduated from high school. The exam was conducted by Panjab University and the results of Matriculation was published in newspaper. All the parents of my friends and my friends were excited to see in the newspaper to see and listen to result of matriculation in school. I did not care to go to school to listen to result as I was myself sure I would pass and only thing I was interested in knowing who came first or second spot in school and in the city. I stayed home and showed no curiosity to find the result from my school. My father finally said," I am going to school to find out your result. "He was only half way to school and he said he heard everybody talking and saying that I made the second position in the major schools of the city and was placed high first division in the university. The school principal announced my name and wanted to honor me for the position I achieved but I was not there. All my friends and other school kids coming from school told my dad. He came home very happy knowing that I got very high marks with first division in Panjab University Matriculation exam. I was happy to.

I started thinking about going to college. A few months later I applied for admission in three prestigious colleges of Panjab State for getting intermediate education. They all accepted me in their F Sc. (Faculty of Sciences) program and gave me free tuition and books for furthering my education. It was hard for my father to afford boarding and lodging in those colleges. He asked me to apply also in local college which was MOHINDERA College of Patiala named after a king of Patiala. The local college matched the offer other colleges and offered free tuition and books for my two years of intermediate college.

Later that year, I started first year of my classes. This was 1959. I got carried away with my past academic successes. I did not pay much attention to studies. I was distracted by coeducation and girls in every class and female professors to teach. I barely passed in higher math which was my favorite subject. I did score high marks in Physics, chemistry and English. I was not happy myself. I was feeling that I have slacked in many ways. I always competed with myself and stayed very friendly with my classmates. My college principal was upset with me. He called me to his office and threatened me to stop and withdraw my free tuition status.

To my good fortune, this never happened. I realized I was just a student and the college would throw me out if I don't perform to their satisfaction. The college broke up for summer vacations. But I was very upset with myself. Nobody in the family knew my problems as no one ever went to real college except my father. I was scared to hurt him as he only saw my achievements so for and never a failure. I started working hard. I started looking for help in math but could not find any. I worked with another drop out or math dropout. By just working hard I caught up what I missed in first year and prepared myself for second year. In final exam of F Sc. (Faculty of sciences) I was second in the college with the high first division in Panjab University. I was still dissatisfied because I did not make to number one. I had no idea who was that boy but I found out that he had Sanskrit in his optional languages and got full marks in that. After I found out I went to my fellow student and congratulated him.

This was 1960 and I had a decision to make, 'what I want to do with my life?"

Some of my brothers would like me to become a doctor and wanted me to go to medical school. Other would want me to go to engineering college and become an engineer. I knew that my parents had no money to spend on my education. They had all their good wishes for me. They wanted me to be successful but had no idea or money to spend on my goals. I could not find any concrete guidance or leadership from my family or friends.

Sam, you have turned ten today. I want to talk about you. I cannot believe how fast your ten years have passed by. Seems like just yesterday. You and I were in your first Columbus house which your mom and dad lived. You were very small and only a few months old. Your dad was away at work. Your mom left us to buy some grocery from a nearby grocery store. Her car broke down in market place parking lot. She called us for a ride back home. You and I drove my truck about 2/3 miles to store. You were so small that I held you close to steering wheel of my truck. You were sitting in my lap and I was wearing safety belt and my left hand was your only safety belt and I was driving with my right hand. You did not cry until you saw mommy in the parking lot standing and waiting for us.

SAM, you are a very strong boy. You have faced many medical challenges in your life and spent lot of time in hospitals and in doctor's office for your problems. You always kept your smile intact which kept us all happy and have been an inspiring force in our family. I know you have joined a soccer team. Next week in your first soccer game I hope I would see you playing. Your game is at 6:30 pm and flight from Florida arrives about 5:30 pm. I want to be there to see you. I am asking your uncle SUREJ to give me ride from airport. We would come directly to your soccer field. Later on your mom called us due to high heat the game has been cancelled and you would not go to game.

Let us go back to our story when I was trying to make some choices about my own career. I was still getting some guidance and information about different directions. After giving some thought, I decided to apply for entrance to Panjab Engineering College which was in Chandigarh, Panjab. I filled out the admission forms. One question asked in the forms was a mandatory requirement of financial support back up of equivalent of Rupees 10,000 minimum. I had no idea how to answer that question. I left it blank. Finally I got a rejection letter based upon in adequate financial assistance and the college was supposed to give preference to backward area students and backward classes students.

Medical was more expensive than engineering at that time in Panjab University. I did not even try or dare to apply in medical college of the state.

This was month of May, 1960. I had not got any admission to any college leading to any profession or even other higher education. My dreams were to go further in my education, but I was very disappointed. Failures were painful but I could not afford to stop living. I started thinking about what I could do at that time. On the other hand the family was going through financial hardship to make ends meet. I had no idea which direction to go. Everyone was trying to convince me to do this and that but I had no idea and could not motivate myself for anything.

I was eighteen years old. I started teaching as a tutor teacher. I started helping high school students as a tutor and got a few tuitions with the help of a few friends. I started making some money. Soon the word went around and within a few weeks my class rose to 40-50 high school students and I was bringing in about six to seven hundred rupees a month. I rented a big school building and named it "Friends College".

I was able to add a few intermediate college students to tutor also. It was just a small group of 5-6 college students which I was tutoring. I was living at home and no expense of my own. My income rose to about thousand rupees a month and started to give my father the money I was making. He started to save money in a bank account. He told me that he would save that money for me to go to engineering college next year. My other older brothers started helping my dad too in household finances. I was getting up at 4:00am and would work until mid-night with small breaks in my day schedule. In about a year my father told me that I made enough money for the first year of my engineering college. I still had no idea how I would pay for rest of the three years of my college which was four years course.

One evening I was going to my evening walk. On the way I met one of my senior college class mate who was already doing engineering in Thappar Institute at Patiala Panjab. We were both walking together and were catching up with each other. I asked him how was he doing in engineering college and how was he affording such high expenditure of engineering college. He told me that he applied for a government loan which was started that year by government. He advised me to apply for loan after I get admission.

This was March of 1961. I applied again for admission to Panjab Engineering College, Chandigarh Panjab India. I got the interview and selection letter in April. My oldest brother Sushi was home for his end of the session school break as he was a high school teacher. He accompanied me to Chandigarh for my interview. I was interviewed by a team of engineering professors and shortly after that the chairman told me that I had been selected asked me to go for medical exam. My brother took me to Medical doctor for medical tests. He also took me to court house for completing some legal papers required by the college. After all the prerequisite formalities were complete we came back to Patiala. All my family was very happy to know about my admission to engineering college.

I had about six weeks to prepare starting my first semester of college. I continued tutoring students even in this preparatory period for about a month. One day one of my girl student named Parvinder stopped at my house. She needed some help in finishing her home work from school. She was accompanied with one of her relative and was another girl. Parvinder introduced me to her saying," She is sister of my sister in law and her name is Baljit and she is a senior in high school at Sangrur, Panjab. She is visiting us for a few weeks. Her nickname is "Doll" in the family." I asked her how old she was. She wished me Namaste (Indian way to greet someone) and said," I am sixteen." I was probably nineteen years old at that time. In India teachers and tutors are respected and she was kind of respectful. She was tall and athletic looking beautiful girl and was looking at me innocently. She further added that I would graduate next year from school. She seemed very easy to talk. I asked her if she would intend to go to college. She said, "Yes". Every time I would ask her about herself, she would smile and give an honest answer.

I felt as if I knew her from my past life but had no words to tell her. I tutored many girls but never felt attracted to anyone. I kept my mind on the job of teaching and on my goal to make money to go to college. A few days later she met me again on a street while I was rushing to tutor somebody and she was going to see her relatives she told me. She asked me if I could help her for a few days in teaching science and math. I said," yes, but next month I shall go to Chandigarh to start my engineering education". I tutored her for a few days. She went back to Sangrur her home place. I went to Chandigarh to start my engineering education. My father packed my suitcase of clothes as this was the first time I was going away from home to live alone. He gave me a check to pay my first year fees to college. As per his directions I paid my first year college fees in one time. I did not have enough money to pay hostel dues and therefore he and I decided that I should stay in Manimajra which was about eight miles from engineering college. My grandparents lived there in an old home which had no electricity yet. They were not in a position to support me in any way. I rented a room next to their house. My older brother Parkash came to live with me and he picked up the rent for the room. Every day I was able to ride my bike to college which was about eight miles from Manimajra. Some days I made two trips to college on my bike in order to keep up with my schedule of classes, workshops and mandatory military training (NCCR) required those days. This was the time when China aggressed India around 1961/1962. Government of India made it compulsory for all college students to take military/rifle training in case of emergency. Due to that I frequently made two trips a day to attend my classes and NCCR training in the evening. My health was great and I was able to do all that by God's grace.

In the meantime Monsoon season started. It would rain very frequently on most days. One day I walked into my class and I was totally drenched and sat in the back during my class. I decided to buy a raincoat to protect myself. Life was very busy and hard at the same time but I was happy as I was proceeding towards my goal. My brother will help me in cooking meals. He worked at Dera Bassi close to Panchkula about 12-15 miles. I was able to finish my first year of engineering in first division.

This was April/May of 1962. I came home for summer vacations. As usual I visited my old students who told me that Doll had come back to her sister Gurpreet.I went to see her at her sister's house and she was home. She told me that she had appeared in her final Matriculation exam and the result would be published in News Paper to night. In India all Panjab University results appear in a newspaper called Tribune. The Tribune is a state wide newspaper in Panjab state and was to be delivered at Patiala city railway station through rail train around midnight. I told her that I would go to railway station to night to check her result. She gave me her roll number to look into the paper.

I along with my friend Hardev went to Patiala Railway Station around midnight to buy the copy of the newspaper. But the paper did not come in that train. We decided to take the same train to Ludhiana, a bigger city where the newspaper was expected to reach earlier than Patiala. Our train reached Ludhiana at about 2:00am. We rushed to the newspaper stand to get a copy of the paper. As all the students were there to buy a copy and it was being sold so fast. Finally I bought a copy and started looking her roll number Doll gave me. I found her number in the list. I was happy to find that she had passed her final exam. My friend and I took train back to Patiala and the train reached Patiala railway station around 6:00 am.

We stopped at Doll's House and conveyed her the good news and congratulated her. She just woke up and was very happy to know that she had passed. I did not know why I was interested in her life. She asked us if we would stop for a cup of tea. But we were so tired and sleepy as we were running around in trains almost all night, I said, "later" She told me that she would want me to stop back and wanted to discuss her further career plans. I told her," I shall stop by in a few days again and we shall talk."

After a few days, I visited her at her sister's house. She was very happy to have mine surprise visit. It was a hot day. She asked me if I would like to have some cool lemonade. I said, "Yes that will be great." She asked her maid servant to prepare lemonade from fresh lemons. We both sat in front of each other on chairs and stated conversation. It was not that easy to find topic to discuss. I only knew how to teach and she was still very young. I ended up asking her," Dolli, what do you want to do? Do you plan to go to college for further education?" She said," I would go to college." I suggested her to go in medical profession like her sister. She told me that she had not studied sciences such as Physics and chemistry. I said," Do not worry. I can help you learning these subjects."

She agreed and decided to join Mahindra College in Patiala. During our conversation, In the meantime the servant lady brought lemonade for us.

Our mutual attraction and interest in each other continued to increase day by day. Her jovial nature and honesty always stuck me. She was always a smiling face and very optimistic about her future. We could not wait to see each other. Those days there were no easily available phones. The only way to stay in touch with some body was to visit in person. Next day I went to see her again. She was as usual very happy to see me. She told me that she had made up her mind to go to college and take medical sciences. But I could not see anything about her that she was worried. She was just a carefree soul. She had no idea that to catch up her missed past education would take some time. I told her next time I would like to see you doing something for preparing for college classes. It was just my way of thinking about her.

After summer she started her college session. I met her almost once a month. She would ask me some help in science classes. I would help her about an hour or two only once a month. She completed her first year in college but I had no idea how she was performing in her scores. Finally she started her second year in college. I always thought she would do well and would finish her premedical at least in passing grade. But in the fall of that year she told me that she could not appear in the university exam as her scores were lower than pass in Physics and Chemistry and she had decided to drop from college of premedical sciences. I was disappointed. But I had no other way to help her in any other way and I was still attached to her in all ways.

She started thinking about other options. She started thinking of her own. Fortunately she found out that the admission to Physical Education College of Patiala under Panjabi University was going on. She applied to that college with a good record of her sports and games during her school and college years. She used her good record in sports such as running races and playing field hockey with many achievement certificates and medals in applying to the college. After an interview and a race competition she was accepted to CP Ed (Certificate of Physical Education) training course. Her family and father agreed with her plan and they paid her fees and she moved from Nabha to Patiala which was about half hour train or bus ride. I went back to my engineering college in Chandigarh. Patiala was in my way during my visits to my home and it was a bus stop close to her college. In this new pursuit she did not need my tutoring help in any way. This was entirely her own interest and determination. She being very athletic and good in sports and devoted herself in Physical Education and started doing great.

There was no pressing reason for us to see each other except there was still some mutual attraction which existed between us. I would see her once or twice a month as I visited my home from my college in Chandigarh just to stay in touch. But there was something beyond that which no one really knew. I was in love with her and I was feeling guilty about falling in love with my student as per prevalent culture in

India. She was a wonderful girl and for me she was real. I could see her selflessness. Even today about fifty year later she is like that. She seems to live for others and love to do things for others. She is only happy if someone else is happy with her actions. She does not seem to put he needs or demand first with anybody and at any time.

I cannot help loving her simply because she is least demanding and never try to manipulate. Most of the time she does what someone else want her to do for them. She help anyone who ask her for help. In process she may do things just ignoring her own health and wellbeing. In our family we all want her to take care of herself also and we do not have any problem in serving others. Her agenda for living sometimes is just others and she love to serve others. She longs to belong to somebody and help somebody.

I know she loves me for reason that I could never understand.

After my summer vacations, I joined second year of my engineering. I was getting tired of living so much away from my college. I moved about three miles closer in sector 20 of Chandigarh. It was about five miles from my college. The work load of study was increasing in second year. Some of my classes were ending very late in the evening and driving bicycle in the dark in traffic was becoming strenuous. Cooking and doing laundry along with study was getting tough. My elder brother was also getting tough time to reach his school in time. We decided to split. He moved to back to Dera Bassi and I applied for Hostel accommodation in college. I got assigned to Himalaya Hostel and on second floor. Life became easier and normal like others in my class.

I was living with my classmates and were able to contact them about homework etc. and vice versa.

One afternoon I did not have classes. I went to recreation room to play tennis. While in the middle of the game, one of my friend came and interrupted the game and gave the message that some guests were waiting for you in front of your room. I said," I am not expecting anyone. Who are they?" He said," Two good looking girls. "I said," I know you are just kidding and want to take my place in the game." But to my surprise in a few minutes I found Baljit and her older sister entering the recreation room and wished me Namaste. I had no idea how they found my Hostel and my room number. I took them to my room. My room was in a mess. Everything was very dis orderly except my books and study desk. Baljit was looking into my stuff in the room, my dirty NCCR uniform which needed wash and there was dusty spots which I did not take time to dust off and actually never noticed being there. She was looking into my everything as if she was on a finding CIA mission about me. Unfortunately she could not find any skeletons in my closet. I kept talking to her sister about her purpose of visit which was her job related for PGI Hospital(Post graduate institute) which was right next to my engineering college. She told me she came to her directorate office for some administrative business and Dolly just came along with me.

In the meantime the waiter knocked the door. He brought the tea and some snacks which I ordered before I left the recreation room. She was looking into my eyes to find out if I was a lie. I had no other girlfriends. I was always honest with her. She finally started believing me. After we all took our tea and snacks, her sister said," it's about our bus time so we should be leaving for bus Stand." I took both of them to bus stand. Bus was ready to leave. As I looked into the bus window Jiti had already taken the window seat. We were both looking at each other. Soon the bus conductor blew the whistle and the bus left and disappeared very fast. I was standing there looking in the direction of the bus route which was nothing but empty space. It was one of those wintery day when moon was in a dark cycle and I was coming back on my bike to hostel which was about three miles from bus stand. I was feeling as if someone very precious came to me and gone in a very short time and had taken something away from me which I could not figure out what. That night I could not concentrate on my studies. Actually even the next couple of days were very difficult for me. I was totally disoriented and could not concentrate on my studies even during my classes. I could not help thinking about her. I never felt that before and thought I was falling in love with her. Just about fourth day I received her letter in mail confirming her love feeling for me. I was happy and got back to my usual study routines.

This was getting close to end of my second year in engineering. I was getting more and more involved with her and rather getting obsessed. She would write me more often as letters were the only way to stay in touch with someone in those days. I started replying her letters too. I was thinking about her even in my classes. My kind of attitude continued in my third year of engineering. I was going home more often and on the way I would see her. One time I stopped at her college Hostel on Friday and it was dark as it was in the evening. I stopped at the gate and a group of girls were coming in their track uniforms after their games or races. I asked a girl where I could see Daljit. She said," Yes she is with us. She was walking in the same group and was a few steps ahead and she called her. "Actually I could not recognize her in her track suite and she just was just two steps ahead of me. She said I could not see you until I let my hostel Superintend know about your visit. She guide me to a guest room where I sat and waited until she came back after about ten minutes. She explained about her hostel rules and visiting hours etc. In that year I visited her probably twice more times. One time she took me to a close by popular Sikh Gurudwara(Sikh temple/church) Dukhnawarn in Patiala for prayers which we both needed to help us. I loved that as I was not a person who would consider the differences in religious places. To me all temples, Gurudwaras and Churches were places to worship God. We both prayed for each other and for staying together. We were getting more and more attached with each other in spite knowing that Indian cast and cultural rules would not allow our marriage.

Finally in my third year of engineering my study was getting tougher and tougher and we were supposed to make selection of our final field of engineering. Although I was working hard and was very serious in my studies but I was also distracted. Some of my subjects were different and I was not good at them. Machine drawing was not my best subject. I was struggling in drawing complicated machine drawings and was not able to keep up with the required scores. First time in my entire education I was placed under compartment in machine drawings subject. I realized the importance of creating drawings in engineering. This type of failure happened to me first time and I was very concerned as I could have lost a year in my engineering graduation schedule. I was very depressed and was always afraid of a failure and missing a year.

But I gathered strength and started working hard on other subjects and gave more emphasis on my compartment subject. In my exam I cleared my compartment in machine drawings but another compartment came in other subject which also was in machine design and drawing. I was still under great pressure to catch up with my studies. I was advanced to my final year of engineering but with a compartment in one subject.

I was going through my stress of final exams. Things were not that great at my college. One of my professors were so mad at me that he threw my stuff through window and challenged me that you would never graduate from this college so for as he was professor in the college. Right those days my personnel life started falling apart. I received a letter from Baljit that said," Our society will not allow us to marry each other as we do have different caste and even different realign. I have no intention of approaching my family as I know they are all set in old traditions of society."

I replied her," We make the society and society can be corrupt dishonest and untruthful at large depending upon times and resources which effected it". We should not let our society make us. Our traditions may or may not be correct in this time and may have to be changed. Society will not change until we change it. This is the truth I believe in. I do not believe in caste system and some of our religious practices and taboos placed on us by society. We are just humans and are in love with each other." She replied back," No. I cannot go against the society rules and traditions and I am sure my family members will certainly will not accept it". I was shattered and depressed. I did not communicate with any one for a few days. Finally one of my friend came to me and asked," What is happening with you Sharma? You are quite and disoriented". I told him the whole story. He got so involved that he gave a telegram to Baljit that I was very sick. Nothing happened. Only thing happened was that Bakjit was worried about me. At least that was what she wrote me in a letter in reply to that telegram.

On my next trip to home I stopped at her college to see her. Things were very tense between us. She told me that some of my family members were very uncomfortable with the idea of her marrying me. At this point they all knew our relationship with each other and had an idea that something serious was going on As usual Ryan your Nanni was placed on a check and restricted movement. She was not allowed to go anywhere alone unless her family members accompany her. She told me that after the training she would go back to Sunam and stay with the family. She also made me clear that she might not stay in touch with me as she felt as if our relationship was a UN achievable goal of her life. She wanted to make a clean break but she did say," You will be my love for this life and she will miss me even if she get married to someone else and somewhere else.

I felt totally rejected and dumped. I could not figure out what was wrong with me and … After that I did not receive any communication from her. This was my final year in engineering school. I tried to concentrate on my studies but was finding very difficult. II was still having problem in clearing a compartment in one subject. I was under great pressure as I knew if I did not clear the compartment and even if passed all other subjects I would be declared as a failure and would lose one final year and had to repeat that year again. This was the first time in four year that my father was concerned and he wanted to know where I studied and what I was doing. One evening he came to see me along with my cousin brother from Burail village. I was not in my room. I was trying to stabilize myself from the break up from jiti. I was gone to Lake Sukhuna which was a recreation spot in Chandigarh, I was gone to do some boating as I was the member of the boating club of the college.

When I came back I found from my friends that my father came to see me. I was very disappointed. My friend told me that he took my father and my cousin brother to dining hall and fed them dinner before they left. My father's visit reminded me what for I was in college and what he expected out of me. Although he never met me that day and did not even say me anything later, yet the incident gave my efforts of studding a blow. I started studding hard to clear and graduate from the college final year as only a few months were left in the final exams.

I lost all contact with Baljit. She finished her physical education training and left Patiala and went to her parents in Sunam. She never communicated with me from there. My mind was still set on her. This was 1965. My life was like a machine. I spent all my life in studies or eating food. I was thinking that I had lost her and I had no idea whether I should continue seeing her or not. I was thinking that our relationship was over and I was simply trying to pick the pieces and tried to devote myself to my studies as I knew that I still had to do that. Although I had no motivation to do anything yet I continued. I devoted all my time to my studies in spite of feeling bored about everything.

I finally took my final exam of engineering degree and also took my catch up compartment in Electrical Machines subject. Although I was very careless about my studies yet I continued whatever was expected out of me. I had no confidence or hope to achieve anything in my academic or personnel life.

This was around July of 1965. One day sitting in Library I found from the newspaper that I had passed in my engineering degree in pretty unexpected high marks and I also cleared my mandatory requirement of passing in electrical machine compartment subject. I was still living with my parents. Everybody in my family was thrilled to know that I had graduated in my engineering education as they all expected. This was the time I felt although I had achieved my goal of becoming an engineer but had failed in my personnel life. She had left me and I was totally frustrated and had no idea how to cope with such condition.

I was spending most of my time in library simply studding newspapers or magazines. I was going out for long walks and wondering what I did to myself. Actually I was just depressed and had no idea what to do. My friend Dev was working and he would see me in the evenings almost every other day.

This was almost later part of August of 1965. My great grand aunt was at death bed. In my life time I never experienced someone that close to death. She had not been well and did not eat anything for days. It was very traumatic experience which I never saw before. It was a process for me to learn how death happens. I was scared. My other family members made her to lie on floor on a sheet which was spread for her. But she was still alive and she always loved us all so much, I could not believe happening to her. She was in her nineties. But her existence and her life always mattered me. I was wondering why …This continued for two three days. This continued and was the fourth day of her lying on the floor and was still alive. This was the time when no doctor had to sign a death certificate, only the family or neighbors made that determination.

My father and mother asked me to read to her the eighteenth chapter of Bhagwat Gita sitting right next to her on a little Indian made pedestal to sit. I did and in a few minutes after that she took her last breath and died. That was what everybody including all the neighbors were telling me would happen. I got involved in her final cremation rites. One of my cousin brother and I went to buy bamboo sticks to make a ladder to take her body to cremation grounds. As in those days' dead bodies were not supposed to be kept overnight unless refrigeration was available to preserve the body. We could lift and carry her body to cremation grounds and cremated her before the end of that day. I was very sad simply thinking about how everybody's life eventually ends.

All this happened when I graduated from engineering college. For me there was no graduation party to attend or even any time to celebrate my success. I was facing the reality of life and death. I loved my great grand aunt. When I was a child she would give me sweets hiding from everybody else. I used to talk to her. I was lost and had no thought of what to do. I had no idea what to do with the engineering degree I earned.

This was the third day after great aunt's cremation ceremony. My father asked me to take her ashes to Ganga Ji – Hardwar. I said Ok but it was very hard time for my father financially. He had no money to give me to buy a railway ticket to Hardwar. He told me to go to my elder brother Jatinder to get some money for railway fare. I took evening train to Ambala and had final remains of my great aunt with me. My brother was employed in a small village as a teacher close to city of Ambala in Haryana. I was told not to take the final ashes of my aunt to the place my brother lived. As suggested I hanged the bag of remains on a tree along the road on my way to the village which was in a public right of way. Then I thought that if someone saw the bag and opened or threw it. As an alternative I took the bag down and kept with me. I reached the village and the house where my brother lived. I secured the ashes of great aunt outside the house in the yard where my brother lived. I met my brother and broke him the sad news of great aunt's death. I asked him to give me some money to buy railway fare to Hardwar. He was stunned hearing about her death.

Next morning as we both (Me and my brother Jatinder) woke up he gave me some money to buy ticket to Hardwar which is a first city where the holy river Ganga flows from mountain to plains and is a great worshiping place for all Hindus. He also gave me some money to donate for the final rites of her ashes at Ganga River. I took the bag of remains and walked back to railway station which was about three or four miles. I took the evening train and traveling all night in train I reached Hardwar (Ganga Ji) in the early morning.

After reaching there, I hired a rickshaw (A tricycle driven by a driver) and asked him to take me to the specific spot (Called KanKhal) where the final remains or ashes of dead peoples were dispersed in river Ganga as per Hindu religion and beliefs. The river was spread a little on the west side at this location. The water was hardly two feet deep but very muddy. I walked through the muddy water about fifty/sixty feet and dispersed in water the final ashes of my great aunt as per Hindu religion. After that with my muddy feet I walked back to the holy bank of river Ganga where traditional bath was supposed to be taken by me as per the family tradition. The water was very cold but clean. I did not take the bath first rather decided to go see my family Hindu priest (Called Panda means Pundit) in Hardiwar. The priest kept a complete record of deaths and births in our family and maintained our family tree of ancestry. He took a comprehensive report from me about our family covering our grandfather and his sister whose remains I took to river Ganga. After he took the information of passing away of my great aunt he updated our family tree. I was highly surprised about his accuracy of maintaining our family tree as he confirmed some information about the past happening to me. He suggested me to go to river Ganga and take a holy bath.

I went to river Ganga Stairs (called Haridiwar Pauri) where I was supposed to take the holy bath but found the river water icy cold. I was thinking if really God wanted us to take this bath he could have warmed the water a little. Therefore I postponed my bath for the later time of the day thinking the temperature might go up and started walking towards North Mountains where the river Ganga was flowing from. I walked about five –seven miles and it was about 1.00 PM as I started walking around 8:30 AM.

The Sun had warmed everything. This was the place where river Ganga was very much levelled and very wide. The water did not seem to be very deep as I saw some saint standing in water and taking bath. The water was to his knees only. I saw him about four or five hundred feet away. I decided to take bath at the spot and no other person was close to me in the river. Actually I could not even see any one even far away in the river. I took my bath in the holy river and felt great, cool and calm. I did not know how to swim, so I sat in water and took a good bath and enjoyed it.

After I dressed myself after my bath, I saw a small hut for away. I started walking towards that. That was a Saints or Sadhu's (Hermit's) ashram or abode. I entered into his cottage and he wished me welcome without saying anything. He was in deep meditation. He did not talk to me much. I wanted to talk to him but he stayed in his meditation and blessed me with his hand jesters. I was confused about what the religion was and had some questions about religion as a young person. I was trying to get some insight about what made a religion. I realized that was not that easy subject and found that you could not learn from …

I walked back to the city of Hardwar and reached Hardwar Pori where people performed all the traditional rituals. I was tired and sat under the shade of a tree. There were some saints already sitting under that tree in their kind of orange color clothing's. They appeared to me some younger sadhus. I wished them Namaste and started conversation with them. I asked them some funny questions about life and death and purpose and the cause of life as I was still grieving about the loss of my family member. They were five of them. They all talked to me and explained to me their experience and belief about death and birth of humans. They did not tell me from where they got their wisdom or belief. But to me they were very comforting and enlightening. They talked to me about spirituality in general without convincing me about any religious beliefs of any particular religion. After spending about couple of hours in their company I invited them all for a dinner at a Dhaba (a small restaurant) nearby. This I did as per our family ritual. They were all total vegetarians and ate two chapattis each (Two picces of bread each) with some lintels which we normally call 'Dal'. I offered and tried to convince them to eat more and any sweet they like.

But they were all together in saying," today you are paying for our food and that does not mean we would eat more. This is what we normally eat and some day we don't eat at all. We are working on staying content with whatever god gives us every day." They taught me to control my needs and stay in limitation about how much I eat. It was very hard thing for me to stick to their advice for food as well as for other things, but I always tried. After feeding them I took a train back to my home town Nabha. Some of these sadhus were not too elderly than me. Next morning I reached my home.

The period of boredom started for me. I had no job and no body to communicate. I turned totally introverted and depressed. I started looking for a job very aggressively as I was feeling very desperate to do something and to earn some thing. I went to Patiala looking for a job in industrial area where there were some electrical manufacturing company. I walked into an electrical switch manufactures factory where different electrical equipment was being manufactured. I applied at that factory and could get a quick interview with the manager and as well as the owner director of the company. This was BeeGee Corporation of Patiala and they were in manufacturing switches, motors and transformers business. The manager agreed to give a job as apprentice engineer on half pay for three months and promised me to advance my salary to full after completing my training/ apprentice period of three months. I accepted and signed a contract as required.

Next day I joined the job and started commuting from Rampur to Patiala which was about 18 miles through bus. The fact was I wanted to keep myself occupied mentally as well as physically to help the family and myself.

At my leisure time especially on weekends I would drift into Dolly.s thought and would feel the pains of separation as I loved her deeply. I did not know how much I had already become dependent and addicted to her. I would be thinking about her almost all the time. I was totally imbalanced and mad about her. I even drew a picture of her in my own eyes. It was not a great picture but my older sister decided to take that picture to her at Sangrur where she (Dolly) lived and gave her. My sister was in favor of our relationship and marriage. But I did not hear from her for long time. She was still trying to work out with her family. May be she was still trying to work out and understand herself what she wanted out of her own life. Weather she loved me or some other avenues she thought were better for her. On my side I was confused and had no knowledge whether she wanted me or something different. My sister came back and did not say anything. I wanted her to let me know and guide me. From her general response I got the message as negative response from Jit. My life continued as an empty vessel. Although I was not very enthusiastic about anything still I continued to get a better job for myself.

During that time, there were some new job openings advertised in newspaper in Panjab State Electricity Board. I applied for that and about a month later I got an invitation for an interview. After the interview I was selected and got an offer. I accepted that and I was appointed at Sangrur as Assistant Engineer and sub divisional officer. My incentive was that Dalit lived only 15 miles away from Sangrur and Dal lived there. I turned in my resignation and notice at BeeGee Corporation which they accepted reluctantly. After couple of weeks of training at Panjab State Electricity Board at Patiala headquarters I joined at Sangrur.

Although in the day mostly I was busy in my apprenticeship training yet I could not get my mind off Jit. Now I was only fifteen miles away from where she was but could not see her. A few time in a month I would pass through town of Sangrur in my field Jeep while looking over my transmission lines but could not see her as I never knew her home address or where about.

I was not hearing about her from anywhere. She would not write me any letter and no message through any source. I was still thinking about her all the time but could not get myself mentally detached from her in spite of efforts. Might be my young age and attachment to her. I was getting nervous, worried and depressed. If I would not have been working probably I could have a nervous breakdown. My overall health started taking a toll and my asthma attacks reappeared. My asthma attacks got so frequent in the day as well as night.

I finally took a long sick leave for indefinite period and came back to home at Patiala for proper treatment. My oldest brother Sushi took me to Ambala city to a well-known chest specialist. The doctor after some tests diagnosed me suffering from TB and lungs problem. He gave me medicines and after two three weeks I felt better and my breathing stabilized. I joined back to my job. It was about four months in my apprenticeship period at Sangrur, my employer Panjab State Electricity Board sent me orders to take charge as Sub Divisional Officer 0f Bhakra Management **Board** Panjab of Stores and transportation under Bhakra Management Board of Govt. Of India. Several stores in BMB such as Moga, Amritsar, Bhakara and Jabalpur Ludhiana were placed under my charge. As I joined there about thirty employees were placed under my supervision.

It was a very interesting and challenging job which was keeping me busy all day. After a long day and working hard I would come to my government provided huge residence and would feel lonely and low. I could not wash away Dolly,s memory out of my brain. Often I would be sitting and thinking about her and wondering what she was doing and specifically where was she. Several months passed and I kept myself busy with friends and with my day to day office work. But my feeling of emptiness and feeling of something missing in my life would not go away.

As I was working my days were short but evenings and nights were longer. Finally I decided to find Dolly.I had no idea where she was. I knew one of her friend whom she mentioned a lot that she was her friend Mohini and always talked about her that she was a school teacher in Sangrur girls' high school and Dolly taught physical education in the same school for about a year. That was what I last heard from Dolly. I wrote Mohini a letter asking if she knew where Dolly was. Mohni received my letter and she gave that to

Dolly. I found out that Dolly was also teaching in High school Lehragaga in a small town near Sunam and was commuting from her home in Sangrur via a bus every day.

After she received my letter through her friend, she decided to reply. I received her letter and she expressed her desire to see me. She also wrote me that she was married to someone in Hissar city in Haryana. I replied that letter and told her that I would like to see her too. In next letter she picked up a place in between Jullunder and Lehragaga which was Ludhiana. She picked up the weekend and the time and place which was railway station of Ludhiana around 10.00 AM.I travelled by train to from Jullunder to Ludhiana that morning and Dolly came from Lehragaga in train to. We were both able to make it in time, and I saw her after about eighteen months. She accompanied by her close friend Urmi. Dolly sounded like matured but same loving soul. We were both happy to meet again but I was little conscious as she said she was married. Because of the weekend we decided to spend some more time together. She wanted to do some shopping for her shoes. Although she acted somewhat distant yet she would look at me with the same loving eyes and her eyes were not lying. But part of her gauge would tell me that she would not want to marry me but had brought her friend along who could marry me as she had the same cast and religion as mine. I was confused and had no way to tell her that I only wanted to marry her.

We were all day shopping and in the evening we all decided to stay in Ludhiana. I started looking for a motel close to railway station. Finally I found one typical Indian two story motel and they had a vacancy. We rented a two bedroom room. One bed was for me and the second bed she shared with her friend. Urmi. On the lower level of this motel there was a market place to eat. I brought some food to eat?

The sun had already gone down and it was getting dark. I did not keep track of time much. I was trying to sleep on my bed. Jit and Urmi were on other bed and still talking with each other. Actually there was no TV in our room as compared to modern times and modern motels. We were all still awake.

Dolly called me on their bed. They literally meant that and we all just wanted to talk. I joined them at their bed. That room was very big. We all three talked and tried to catch up with each other. I could not help kissing Jit off and on and she did the same as during the day we were just shopping around and talking around. Urmi watched both of us and concluded that we were just desperate lovers. In my mind I was questioning myself why I was getting involved with a married women. She was also telling me that Urmi was not married. In my mind Dolly was married and Urmi was not. I was getting confused. Finally I checked my watch. It was 2:00AM. I went to my bed and wanted to sleep. I knew I had to go back to my job as my job was 24/7 job. I noticed that Dolly was tired too. I went to sleep and Dolly and Urmi went to sleep too.

I had no idea when the sun arose but I was up. And woke both of them at 7:00 AM next morning which was Sunday. We all got ready and went down where shops were and eat some Purri-Chollas. (Chick Peas and fried bread like tortillas which is very common food available in India as Hamburgers in USA).

Around 10: AM, we were all at the railway station where two trains were on schedule to reach within a few minutes. One train to Lehragaga towards south and other one to north to Jullundur. Lehragaga train which Dolly and Urmi was to take came first. Urmi and Dolly took that train and were both gone in a few minutes and I saw them off. The train I was supposed to take was running delayed and I was standing on the platform and trying to figure out the meaning of last twenty-four hours of my life. I was simply lost as if my whole life was gone and disappeared in front of my own eyes. I was still wondering what was attaching me to only one person out of about 6.7 billion living on this earth. Is this my past Karma or what. Why I feel why I cannot breathe without her?

I reached Jullundur back a few hours later, but I was carrying her with me in my mind. At one moment I would think to one thing and next moment something else. I had no idea what to do with my personnel life but in the office I could perform my duties and responsibilities without any problem.

A few days passed by. It was about 11:00 AM and I was working in my office. The mail man entered my office and said," SDO (Sub Divisional Officer) sahib! I have a personnel letter for you". I thanked him and he left. I opened the letter and found that was from Dolly. In that letter she admitted that she was never married and she just lied. I was overjoyed. I sent her the reply back saying that next time you would come to Jullunder. After couple of months she and Urmi made their trip to Jullunder on a weekend. They wrote me ahead of time about their schedule and train arrival.This time I picked them up from Jullunder railway station in my office Jeep as I was about 3miles away from where they arrived. I booked my rest house and had them stay over there which was only a few hundred feet from my official Government provided residence. Dolly stayed in the rest house and Urmi came to stay at home. I stayed in the rest house with her up to almost 2:00am next morning. We loved each other but avoided sex. It was like old days we used meet each other in Patiala She again told me that if I would marry Urmi which was accepted by the society, she would keep on seeing me. I was confused and had no idea how to handle the situation. Urmi was very nice but in my mind the commitment was done long time ago. I could not change my mind. I understood that she was just saying these things under their family pressure and was not what she actually wanted for herself. I could read that her words were coming from the compulsion of the family and society which she was not planning to fight with as a girl. The caste system and religious differences were in between us in spite of no legal barriers. I was prepared to fight. Two days later the weekend was over and Dolly and Urmi went back to Lehragaga where they were both working and living.

About a week later I got a letter from Dolly. I was invited to visit her in Lehragaga on the weekend. Only train going to Lehragaga was very late at night. I took the train on the late Friday evening and I was in her town around mid-night. It was dark at the railway station. No one got down there when the train stopped. It was only me. I got out of the railway station and started looking for a Riksha to ride to the town. It was a deserted place and on the top of that was a pitch dark. I had no idea how far the actual town was. Finally I found a Riksha standing a few hundred feet away and I walked towards that. I found that the Riksha driver was sleeping in it. I woke him up and he agreed to take me to town. Driving through a few streets and a road without any lights, the driver took me to the address I gave him. The address was not much descriptive except two teachers Dolly and Urmi living in town. It was a small town and the driver new about the town and its people. He asked from one passerby who gave him the directions. In next a few minutes he stopped at the house they lived in.

The driver knocked the door. The door was opened by a man who owned that house and he confirmed that school teachers Dal and Urmi lived in that house also. His family was sleeping in the first room on their cots. They asked me to jump over the cots and go to the next room through an open space. Finally Urmi came and took me to their side of the rented house. They had two beds in their room. I slept in Dolly,s bed and she slept with Urmi. Next day it was Saturday. We all woke up late and spent the day talking. Saturday night Dolly came to my bed to sleep which was actually her bed. We loved each other but abstained from any sexual contact. Next morning I was supposed to catch the train back to Amritsar. A funny thing happened. A guy stopped to see me at their house. He came and asked me to go with him for a talk. After we both came a few hundred yard away from the place they (Dolly and Urmi) lived he said," This is our village. I suspect that you have an illicit relationship and these girls are nothing but conducting prostitution." I told him that he was mistaken and had no idea what was going on. He tried to threaten me but to no avail. He was simply acting like a DON of the town.

As per my schedule I left for Amritsar via next train. Dolly and Urmi started visiting me about a month or twice a month at my place in Amritsar. Dolly applied for a job in Jullunder to work in a school. She got the job with a slight influence from one of my friend. She joined in Jullunder as a physical education teacher in Jullundur High School. She rented an apartment in a house close to her school. She was able to come to see me almost every weekend via bus which was about twenty five miles. Her family started suspected her intentions. One weekend her father and her auntie gave a surprise visit to her and wanted to know what was going on with her. They wanted to take her back to Sangrur. The same evening I went to see her at her apartment UN announced. But before I entered her apartment she noticed and came out and told me that her father and auntie were there and asked me to go back. But to my great fortune I could see my future to be father in law and his sister from a distance. That was the only contact from for away I ever had with Dolly's father. To me looking from how he was dressed and walked he sounded very religious and traditional. I came back to my Kothi (An officer's residence for government officer in India).

A few weeks later Dolly resigned her job and left Jullunder and went back to Sangrur to look after her family. Her father was suffering from heart disease and had no idea how long he would live.

Sam! Today is your 14th birthday. I called you and also sent you an email. But could not get a response from you. Perhaps you were busy. It is ok, nana understands you. You are struggling for little things every day It is not your fault and certainly nobody else but I am always proud of you and you are the beacon of light to our family and teach us all about all mighty. We are very thankful to God who gave us such a nice and lovely grand child who gave us all immense happiness. I missed you. I wish you a happy birthday and hope you had great day. I am sitting alone in my apartment and missing you and everybody else in our family.

SAM, let us go back to My Story. It was about two weeks since your nanny left Jullunder. She wrote me that she was struggling with her family members to convince them to our marriage but to no avail. Her younger brother Mali was too much opposed to our marriage. He told her that your marriage could not happen. He said," As sky and earth can never meet same way you and Kishi cannot meet and marry each other".

Dolly lived in restrictions and a strict watch. She was not allowed to go anywhere alone. She was getting frustrated and depressed from her circumstances and did not know what to do. This was 1968 March and just the first week. India was not only backward but caste system and religious divide in the country was very dominant and there was no laws being enforced on these kind of issues. Although country had been free and independent for the last twenty one years but people's views and thoughts were not free. Inter caste and inter religion marriages were few and far between. Society was highly conformed in their ways.

I was sitting in my office and was busy as usual in my sub divisional office work. The mailman walked into my office totally UN announced and handed over a letter from Dolly. It was about third or fourth march. I opened the letter. She wrote," I am coming to you on 9th March and this is forever. If you would not need me I would go on somewhere else and will never see you again". I was happy but had no idea what to plan or reply. I knew that it would be unlawful to keep her with me without our marriage. I talked to one of my close friend and explained him the whole situation and asked him to find someone who could marry us like a Hindu priest. He went to a temple on my behalf and asked a priest if he could perform the marriage. He came back and told me that the priest would not marry us until the parents were in presence in the temple. This was not possible from both of our family.

Then I talked to one of my Sikh friend about our marriage problem. He said," Let me go and check with a Sikh Gurudwara, s priest to marry us. He was very confident that he would marry us as the priest came from serving Indian military and was highly broad minded". He finally made an appointment with that Sikh Priest for marrying us on 9th march evening, exactly the day Dolly was supposed to come to me.

I arranged a car to pick us from my Kothi (A government provided delux Residence), but I had no idea what time she would arrive. First car came and waited for an hour and left. She was not in Jullundur yet. At about 4:00PM train reached the Jullundur Kent Station and jiti made in that train. She took a Riksha to my office at grid substation. A second car was waiting at my Bypass road office and residence for us. As soon as Daljit arrived she took a few minutes to freshen up and get ready to go. I told her the marriage plan and my oldest sister accompanied us. At about 6:00 PM we were in Gurudwara close to railway station Jullundur. My friends Sidhu, Saini and Hans were already waiting for us. On 9th March, 1968 about 7:00PM we were married according to Sikh rites in that Gurudwara in presence of my friends and my eldest sister who was in favor of our marriage. Right after the ceremony, the car dropped us at the close by Jullundur railway station at about 7:45 PM to catch a train to Delhi as planned. We both caught the express train to Delhi. It was about 8:00 PM, the train whistled and our friends wished us farewell and we were on our way to Delhi.

We took a sleeping berth in the railway train compartment. We slept on the same berth but slept with our feet towards each other. It was long train ride. Next day at the day break we were at Delhi. I had no reservation at any place. I told the Riksha driver to take us to any hotel he knew was good to stay in. We checked in a hotel in the morning of 10th march. We were both tired of travelling at night. We both decided to take shower and go to bed. First time after long time we loved each other without any fear as we both knew that we were married to each other at that time. After a few hours of love and then rest we went to eat our lunch at a nearby restaurant. After eating our lunch we went to bed again. Next day we sent a telegram to Dolly's parents in Sangrur that we had married happily and we were ok. We spent about 2-3 days with the same routine of eating and went back to sleep. That was our honey moon and some time we would worry and fearful that someone might follow us and might try to harm us in one way or other. We were not only fearful from our own families but also from people on the street who believed in only in traditional as well as cast compatible marriages as we were being threatened from unknown people and sources.

We spent about 2-3 days like this and kept our routine every day. On about fourth day, one of my friend found out that we were married and were in Delhi. He called me and came over to our hotel and insisted on taking us both to his two bed room apartment. He knew that we were hiding from our families and were in a need to hide until the things calm down. He was living alone and had a servant to cook his food. The servant was very happy and nice to have us over. He would happily cook for us and our friend. Every morning he would make us a breakfast of scrambled eggs and parathas stuffed with potatoes. His special breakfast menu almost every day became our permeant favorite treat. Even today after about forty eight years later Baljit (Dolly) like to prepare this breakfast of scrambled eggs with tomatoes, onions and green papers. Our whole family always loved it.

We stayed with our friend for about a week. I had to call my boss to get my four day leave extended. We decided to stay in Delhi and do some site seeing. Next morning we hired a motor Riksha to see all the historical and other worth seeing places in Delhi and Bombay. The motor Riksha driver was also a great tour guide. One of the most interesting place we visited was the actual home of Late Prime minister of India 'Lal Bahadur Shastri'. His widow (Mrs Shastri) gave us a tour of her small house. We were very surprised and impressed by seeing the working home office of the late prime minster who sat on an Indian carpet spread on the floor and had a low level wooden table in front of him to write his official notes. Mrs Shastri showed us the glass and a pitcher made of copper and brass which he used to drink water. She blessed us in an Indian way as she gathered from our conversation that we were recently married and were on our kind of honey moon and we both touched her feet. Next interesting stop of our visit was famous Birla Mandir(A Hindu Temple) as the guide showed us the exact spot and the compound where Mahatma Gandhi,the father of the nation was assassinated during India's partition. Seeing some of the old historical buildings like Red Fort, Qutab Minar, and Ashoka Pillar was very enlightening for me as an engineer as they gave the proof of centuries old knowledge of engineering and architecture of Mughal times of India. During our visit of gardens we also took a ride on an elephant which was our first and the last ride on an elephant.

Finally after about ten days my official leave was coming to an end and on March 20th, 1968 we said good bye to Dehli by a bus. The bus route was along GT road to Panjab. One of the city on our way was KURU KSHETER in Haryana state of India. My older brother lived and worked there. As the news of our marriage was still very raw to our family in Sangruer as well as in Patiala and we were not sure about the reaction of our family members, I talked to my brother to keep Baljit with him for a few days until the matter cooled down for her safety. I left Dolly in Kuru Ksheter and went to my job in Amritsar.

I spread the news at my office and in my locality that I got married during the vacations I took in last ten days. I could not disclose more details about our marriage like where and when etc. My elder sister who attended our wedding and was living with me at that time told me that my brother in law and Dolly's nephew came looking for us both. She said," I told them that you were gone on a vacation to Simla, a famous city of Himachal Pardesh known for vacations. They went back to Sangrur. I stayed about couple of weeks then visited Dolly in Kuru Ksheter. I could not stay away from her and neither could she as she told me via a letter. After about six weeks things started calming down at her home. The family in Sangrur told people in town that Baljit was married by her older sister Gurpreet and had gone to live with me in Amritsar.

I brought Dolly back to Amritsar to live with me and my sister. In the last week of April, 1968 we were both together in my residence. We were married legally but in people's eyes we were just living together as they did not see any ceremonial wedding as they did in India those days.

…

In around June Baljit told me that she was feeling different and might be pregnant. I took her to a lady doctor who confirmed her condition that she was pregnant. She was very excited and so was I. But on the other hand she was very much worried about many things. She was still nervous about the situation at her house and at my house too. About three and four months had elapsed since our marriage. No one in our both family had accepted our marriage. India is a country where social acceptance is more prevalent and important than legal acceptance of things. The people in neighborhood would question us about our marriage and would indirectly try to pry and ridicule us asking details of our marriage. Even my own father was upset with us both because we married the way we did and she (Baljit) was not invited to our home.

This was the time when we were both dedicated to each other. I could not stay away from her and she was feeling the same way too. She started throwing up and it was being confirmed that she was pregnant. She was throwing up about six times a week. I had no experience of such problems. She told me that she felt throwing up every time she saw me. I said to myself," Am I so ugly or what?" I took her back to Gynecologist who told us she was pregnant initially and she told us that she could do nothing and again confirmed that she was pregnant.

Sometime in August of that year Baljit got very sick. I asked her what happened. She said," I was trying to sow some clothes myself for our future baby. I needed the sowing machine for that. I picked up the sowing machine for that and since then I had a severe pain." My education about such problem was very limited. I simply loved her and could not see her in in pain. At the same time I was very dedicated to my job and went office to do what I was supposed to do.

Her pain became unbearable. She sent a message to me through a servant that she wanted to see me pronto. I immediately came home. She was in a deep pain and could not even talk and explain what she needed. I told the servant to get hold of driver and ask him to bring the jeep. Just in a few minutes the driver came in the jeep and asked him to take her to Jullundur hospital. On arrival to hospital a woman doctor checked her promptly and said that she had aborted a baby and she needed to be admitted in the hospital and undergo surgery what they called curating. Baljit was in severe and terrible pain and I could not see her face in pain. The nurse brought some papers to me to sign for her surgery and I signed. She was taken in for a surgery for some surgical procedures. After about couple of hours of my anxiety doctor came and came to talk to me about her condition. He told me that sometime in the evening she would be released to go home. The doctor explained to me what happened and told me to take care of her.

Almost in the evening, sun was going down and it was getting dark and clouds were shadowing. I brought Jit home to my Kothi, my residence provided by government. We were both sad that we had lost our first baby. But I was relieved as my darling Baljit was not in pain any more. She was in peace and in comfort. I had no idea why that also made me comfortable and happy. A few days later she gained strength to get up and work around. Until then she was feeling dependent on servants to do everything. She was not liking to get everything done by servants. She wanted to cook mine and her food herself. In spite of me telling her not to do anything and just take care of her health, she started cooking and doing some light work by her own will.

Couple of months had gone by. She was feeling stomach problems, and complaining about her belly ache almost all the time. She was not good with allopathic medicine, so I took her to an Arya Vedic medicine doctor. Some way after feeling her pulse he told her that she was grieving and unhappy about the abortion and wanted to keep that baby and never thought of losing that baby. He asked me to stay more close to her.

I started devoting more time to her. We would go to movies almost every week end. We would go out for walks in the evening and connect with each other. I found out that was too busy with my own job and responsibilities and were neglecting her needs. We started socializing more with my colleagues and diverted ourselves away from problems. Both of us were very much consumed with worries about what our family members were thinking and would do or behave with us. Both of us were getting to the point to ignore our own welfare and happiness and we were both suffering as for as our own health was concerned. Life was great but our concern of our own families and society was still plaguing us both. Neither of us were so selfish and maintained our regards for the family as well as society as a whole and behaved very calmly in every situation and interaction with everyone.

Just in a few months, Baljit was pregnant again. This time she was happy and were not worried about anything. Some of the new signals for me were different. She was very happy. She wanted to have this baby and she had already fallen in love with this baby. She was taking care of herself good as per doctor advised her. I had no idea what she was going through. She started throwing up again and started being very un-comfortable again. I was thinking what a woman had to go through to have a baby. Although I was concerned about her health but was very excited and wanted to be a dad. We both decided that we would not name our own children and let our friends and relatives name them whatever they would want.

SAM, on May 28th, 1969, your mom and my first and foremost child was born in the late hours of evening. We were at a private hospital and a private doctor named Sandra Devi who delivered your mom. She was a prominent Jullundur/ Amritsar Gynecologist who practiced from her home. There was a tradition those days that dad would put honey on new born baby's tongue. Your Nani#2 Nimmi was with us and she had me stick to that tradition. I was supposed to do that. I was supposed to do that with my finger and not with spoon. I went to the bathroom and rubbed my finger with soap on the hard floor made of stones as I was almost hysterical about germs. After I felt somewhat confident that my fingers are not contaminated I touched honey to your mom's tongue when she was just taking it out with her high pitch voice of crying. As soon as I touched honey to her mouth she became calm and started sucking that honey.

We had not yet named her. My friends came to the hospital to congratulate us and were very happy to see the new baby.

Urmi asked me to go with her to market which was not too far to get some essentials for the baby. I and your Nani#2 went to a market which sold all kind of new baby stuff. She picked some Johnson and Johnson soaps and skin creams for your mom. I had no idea what she was buying as I never bought anything even for myself. I paid whatever she wanted me to pay for. For me that was the good part of life I did not have to know everything and simply trusted someone to make that decision for me and I always knew that it was very hard for me to make small and routine decisions. Your Nanni and I were still had no idea to name your mommy. We were both like we would decide when the time comes. Urvi Nanny decided to name our first baby as NEERJA which meant in our language a lotus flower born out of water. Sam, your mommy is that Neerja (a lotus flower) AND VERY Komal but after your birth she had proved us and the world that she is much more than that. She is your mom.

SAM, I am going to tell you more about her I know she would not want me to. You know that she is your mom and I know that she is my daughter and we both love her and that is our greatest connection.

Just about ten days after she was born, she got some stomach ache. She was almost going to die with that. Her eyes were pale and were not even blinking. We got worried about her health and questioning whether she would survive or not. We took her to a Boarder Security forces Surgeon. The doctor told us that protect her from any germs or infections or contaminated milk etc. He gave some antibiotics and medicine worked and she survived. She had bad stomach virus which she got over with medicines. A few months later she was walking and talking and was still less than a year old. She might be nine or ten months old. She became so active that she would be running around with so much energy that I never could imagine.

For me life had changed. I never had that kind of pleasure in my life. She would accompany me to my office. She was so friendly with everybody she would see on our way. She called me 'Pappa,Pappa'. All my office people loved her. She had no fear about anything. Anyone in my office and on the grid substation would pick her and she would go with them. Now she was walking and running. She could go and crawl under fences and would go to my friends. She knew exactly in which house quarter they lived. They all loved her to have her. She would come to my office and sit on the table and would play with my phone and would ring official bells to call my peon without any reason.

Sam, I am talking to you about your mommy. Sam smiled and was very happy to know and hear about his mommy. I got so much attached with her from the day she was born that I would come home from my work and pick her and play with her. I always felt very happy to spend time with her after my own stressful life. My ears would long to listen someone say," Papa, Papa". No one knew that that was the best part of my life and no one the secret of my high energy at work.

Once in a while someone will make a remark," See when you don't follow and obey the parents and family, you get girl instead of a boy". This was the time Indian cultures always preferred boys over girls. It probably still is in India that prefer to have boys than girls. Does India still disseminate between Boy and a Girl, right from the day they are born? I simply wonder.

In my own mind, I would always think," how ignorant and rude these people are even if these people were born in the same mother land and a land of Godly Rishis and Yogi's and spiritual leaders of India. The happiness to have and cherish a child is a real happiness. The boy or a girl never marred my happiness and never distorted my thinking. The boy or a girl is equally a child to feel happy about. These kind of remarks would touch Baljit very deeply and she would say," I tortured my parents and family and that was why I got a girl as my first baby. In spite of all that she would take care of her like her most precious thing in world. She would give her beauty treatments on her face in spite of every one would say," She is very beautiful and cute." But my neighbors always blamed on my own 'Karmas'. Please feel free to read the holy book of "Bhagwat Gita" of Hinduism to understand the meaning of "KARMA'

Finally in October of 1969 at Diwali festival my family wanted to see her and my father invited Jit home and he expressed their desire to see their granddaughter. We all went to our home in Nabha and Patiala. Everyone in our neighborhood came to see us.

My younger sister took Komal to neighborhood and did not come back for 2-3 hours, when they returned, Komal was so hungry and wanted her mom for her feed. Our life was happy and great. I gained strength to fight and face the society which was very much set in customs and traditions. Off and on someone would make a remark," Who will marry his children? Even if this Neij is a beautiful daughter who would marry her due to their (Mine and Baljit) inter caste and inter religion marriage. Although we were getting discouraging comments about our marriage, yet I and Baljit were very happy and close. Some evenings we all three would go for a walk and Komal would walk and run in front of us like a free bird and no fear of any hunters around, Our life was content. This was the happiest time of our lives.

This was almost January or February of 1970. One morning, Baljit said, "I am not feeling good. I asked her jokingly if this was anything to do with me or something I did. She replied, "Yes". Finally she said probably she was pregnant. I said," Do not worry. This is the best news." Baljit replied that she was very scared and afraid. I asked her what was bothering her, she was looking so beautiful and I loved her in that stage.

Baljit said," I am afraid and I may get another girl." I said," What is a big deal? Komal has brought us so much happiness. Another daughter may bring us more happiness and great luck".

Baljit felt depressed. Some people's voices still rang in her years," You got a girl because you did not listen to your parents and disobeyed them". Baljit was very uneasy. She told me that she would not be able to take care of this baby alone because I was planning to leave India and go to USA. Although I told her that I would not be leaving the world and I intend to take care of our children where ever I would go, yet she would not believe me. I even told her that this baby might be a boy she was looking for. She said," I know how I feel and I want an abortion." Against my own will she convinced me to go to the same Gynecologist doctor who delivered Komal.

The doctor was very nice. She invited us in her office and had us sit across from her office chair. Her name was Dr. Sandra Devi and very prominent doctor of that area who had her own private hospital in her huge house. Baljit said to her, "My husband is leaving for USA and I shall not be able to take care of this baby alone and I want to have an abortion." The doctor said in an angry tone," Mr Vatas, I know you are an electrical engineer. I suggest you to take an electric wire and wrap around her neck if you are agreeing with her for this abortion." I told the doctor that I had no problem but she insisted to visit you and this was her own idea. The doctor explained us the health consequences of an abortion. She even told Baljit that she would take care of her delivery and advised her against abortion. We both came back home. I told Baljit that this might be our most lucky baby. Baljit said," I hope so and may be God will help us". I agreed.

Sam, On January 10, 1971 my most beloved star was born and she happened to your auntie Dipika. I had no special ambition for a boy or a girl but your mom had already taught me how great and beautiful it could be to have just another baby. Before this my life was nothing but a stuck. My health was very bad and my confidence was way too low to continue and face problems I was going through. All of a sudden my life started changing with a force like a tornado change the landscape of the territory it goes through. The best thing happening for me was everything was uplifting and in positive direction. Something developed in me that started giving me power to make decision which I was postponing. In my life or I actually had no confidence to make on account of fear.

SAM, your" mossy or auntie Dipika" was born. She was delivered by the same doctor Sandra Devi who delivered your mommy but in a different room. She was the same doctor who told your Nanni and me that you should not have an abortion. Dr. Sandra Devi had her own private hospital with just a few rooms in her own house. She was a private medical practitioner at Jullundur and Amritsar area of Panjab, India.

Your Nanny and I brought your mom home. Your mom was only a year and half old but she was very happy to have her to play and boss her around. She would never let her cry until she was hungry. Your mom would remind your Nanni to feed her every time she would cry. Sam, it looked like she fell in love with her little sister Dipika and always rebuked us in her little voice to not let her cry and give her anything she wanted.

The news of a new baby arrival finally spread around in the neighborhood and in our Power Station colony of Bhakra Management Board of Govt. Of India. But to our surprise no one out of our neighborhood showed up at our residence Kothi to congratulate us. That was very normal for an Indian society those days that they would not welcome girls in the family. They thought the girls were born and bring ill luck to their parents and family. For me and your Nanni, it did not make any difference. She was a baby we both loved the same way as we loved our all other children. Your mom was so much fascinated with her that she would dictate us how to pick her.

Some of our family members said," When you disobey parents you get only girls as children. None of them had any idea what was going on with our lives and in our luck and how much our two girls were giving us happiness.

No one knew what was happening to our luck at that time. It was changing like a dark cloud becomes bright all of a sudden with a Sun light all around it. We had not even named her yet. Peoples around us were making us feel as the result our own bad Karma which I never believed in. After a day or two I was visiting my friend. He suggested her name to be Madhunicka which meant sweet baby. We both agreed and thought a little and decided to name her Dipika NISHA SHARMA. Dipika Nisha meant a sweet night. Every time I would pick Dipika, Komal would correct me like a guardian saying," Dad hold her like this. She is very small" She was overwhelmed with her coming into the family. Komal had no idea that they were both very small for me. I never saw or heard such love between two little sisters.

This was early 1971. Just a month ago, on December 12th, 1970 I received a permanent immigrant visa from US

Embassy in New Delhi and I was convinced in my own mind that Dipika is a very lucky to our family and especially for me. But my health was in bad shape and my asthma was getting worse and worse. I was having attack after attack and no medicine was helping me. My brother Mani asked me," How you would survive in USA alone in such ill health condition". He was perfectly right and that was also my biggest fear. I started thinking about returning the visa to USA embassy. On the other hand I had already spent all the money I had on my illness. Baljit wanted me to live and she took me to every possible doctor she thought might cure me and spent our whole money. We were broke and I had no money to leave India and go to USA. On the other hand my family members wanted me to cancel the plans and stay in India. I wrote a letter to US Embassy if I return the visa now due to my circumstance and wanted later what policy would dictate. I got a reply that you would be placed in a different priority list and you would lose your current place.

At the same time I got a call from my travelling agent asking me to buy the air ticket to USA. He knew that I had visa to USA. I told him that due to lack of money I could not buy ticket right now and would like to postpone my move. He told me that my visa was for four months and he would sell me ticket through 'Fly now and pay later scheme provide by Swiss Air'. After a few questions I agreed. The travelling agent sent me agreement forms for that. These were the forms which needed to be cosigned by two persons having enough income or property to pay back the air ticket loan.

I asked one of my work colleague whose son was planning to come to USA about my situation. He told me that his son who was a young mechanical engineer was also going to USA. He told me that he would sign anything because I wanted my son to be around someone I could contact in case he needs any information about his whereabouts and welfare. He said," My son will go to USA and can have friends of his own but I would not have any friends who would know me. I want you to go with him to USA. That way, I can always contact you about him. I shall cosign your ticket loan. I let him sign my loan forms. I told him I would be sending my loan installments from USA.

I was needing the second cosigner also. For that I talked to one of my friend who was just a few years younger than me but he was also coming to USA. His name was Dev. He liked me because I would let his dad come to my office quite often and use my phone for his urgent calls. He said to me," We shall live together until your family joins you. My uncle is a village Mayer and owns lot of land in the village. I shall ask him if he could cosign your loan". I said," How he would sign my loan as he does not even know me'. Dev said," Don't worry. I shall introduce him to you. He is an alcoholic and drinks from morning to evening. If you can afford to pay his liquor bill for one day, he will cosign your loan in court as needed. On the whole he is a wonderful guy and very helpful to people."

Next day I along with my friend and Dev went to the court of Magistrate. My friend Tony went to liquor store on my behalf and bought a bottle of whisky. He came back and started serving the drink to Mayer right in front of the court house at about 10:00AM. By 11:00Am the Mayer drank all the bottle. In the meantime the Magistrate had to leave to attend some higher court meeting with a session judge. He did not give us any appointment to see him either. That was the way those days the Indian beaurocracy worked those days. When he came back to his office, it was 2:00 PM. My friend Satish had already served the Mayer two bottles of whisky. After the two bottles were finished, the Magistrate showed up in his court and we took the drunk Mayer to his court to cosign papers in front of him as required. The Mayer was staggering but knew exactly what he came for to the court and was to cosign my loan papers. The magistrate asked the Mayer," Do you agree and support the document you are signing? If so sign here ". The village Mayer signed the loan document of my loan. I was happy to complete the paper work of my loan and I mailed those papers to my travelling agent in Chandigarh. Before getting out of the court, I thanked my friend Tony and Dev. I also thanked the village Mayer but he was too drunk to know anything going around him and we took him in my Jeep to his house in his village of near Phagwara.

After about three four days, my travelling agent called and confirmed that he had received the agreement in order. He said, "You would receive Swiss Air ticket for your travel to USA. Please let me know the exact dates you would want to travel". I was very happy to know that my financial problem was solved. I credited this good luck to my new daughter. I believed that my second daughter would solve my problems because she was born in our all kind of problems.

But my happiness did not last too long. Next morning at about 11:30 AM at my Kothi residence the call bell rang. I came out and there was our mailman. He wanted me to sign for a registered letter. I signed and opened the letter. The letter was from Panjab Engineering college loan department and was signed by the principal. The letter disclosed that the department had learned from a reliable source that I was planning to leave the country for USA without paying in full my education loan which I borrowed during my engineering education.

I was wondering who their reliable source was. In my mind I was still un sure about whether I would go or not as I had not solved my problems about my family and my job with Gov. of India who had never permitted me and never gave me any no objection certificate as required.in my own mind I was still trying to make a decision of my life direction. Some nights I would not be able to sleep all night thinking what, who and where my family would live and survive without me around them if I left for USA.I had a great job but my problem was how the society at that time was treating us due to our inter caste and inter religion marriage. The words of Dr. Sandra Devi was still ringing in my ears," You can still go to USA and kill your wife with an electric wire around her neck being an electrical engineer". I was puzzled thinking who would keep my wife and two daughters in India while I would be gone to USA. I was concerned about the safety of my family.

I had no confidence that my health would cooperate in USA.I had no way to know that I would get a job and would adjust to new conditions in a new country and in a new environment. I was almost twenty seven and everything I wanted to do was for my small family and I was totally suffering from anxiety and asthma. I was getting more and more attached to my wife and mostly with my two little daughters. Every moment I would doubt my ability to cope without my wife and my two lovely daughters. Although I knew that I would get my family over there as soon as I could, yet I was scared with my own direction of my life. With all these doubts, I was still struggling to make a decision of what I should do. Should I go or not. But the letter from the government college was based on because I had a passport and a visa. On the other hand I was not running away from my responsibility of paying my loans which I could have paid from anywhere. I had no intention to do that as I had not decided about such things and relinquish India's citizenship yet. Further the letter I received said," If the loan amount is not paid in full immediately the department will write to passport officer to cancel the passport and would do all other proceedings to block your departure to USA.

I felt like a criminal. I was not planning to stop making payments to my loan even if I would have left for USA.I wanted to know the truth about who was the reliable source to disclose the plans which I had not even decided. I got curious and wanted to resolve the situation. No one exactly knew that I might go to USA except one or two of my family members and one friend whose son was planning to go to USA.

Next morning, I took a bus from Jullundur to Chandigarh and I was in Chandigarh about 11:30 AM. I took a Riksha to my engineering college. Right after the lunch break I was able to see the engineering college loan clerk. I knew that clerk as I dealt with him during my stay in engineering college for many other problems. He knew me for years as he was from the same village of Panchkula where I lived and was from.

From my brief case I took the letter out and showed him. He immediately acknowledged that he initiated and wrote that letter. I asked him how he knew that I might leave the country and go to USA. Right away, he said," Your oldest brother Sushi came and told us in person that you were planning to leave the country without paying the loan". I told him the truth that I had not make up my mind because the decision to hard to make because of my personnel circumstances. I told him that I had a three week old daughter and a year old daughter and wife to take care. I told him that I would give him written statement that in case I decide to leave the country I would pay my loan in full before leaving the country. He agreed. I gave him the written statement as he needed and I left.

During my return journey in bus, I could not help thinking about my family. I was thinking how a real elder brother could do such an act of distrust with his own younger brother. I could not believe that the same brother brought me to the engineering college for admission and never doubted my intentions. Now he could not believe me because I married without family's permission. Six week ago I put my whole trust in him. He was visiting me along with my sister in law during school summer vacations. I enjoyed their stay with me. I disclosed my tentative plan to go to USA when we were just talking face to face during their stay. I always regarded him as my oldest brother and he was many time a guide to me I simply accepted the circumstances. All this was part of me and my own brother, s trust in me. I could understand the implication of my education loan and his fear of him paying all that in case I would had not been responsible to clear that pay the loan from USA. Thinking this being just a family and they would find out any way some day if I do leave for USA. Due to all these problems, I was giving a second thought to my going abroad.

At about 9:00PM I reached home and told her my whole day story to my wife Doll. She was still very encouraging and comforting and told me that she would be with me through thick and thin. The life's ups and downs were not over yet. Nothing seemed to be calm around me and my intuition was saying something else was coming for which I did not plan yet. Next day I received my job transfer orders to receive charge at Fridabad and report to an executive engineer in New Delhi. I was thinking very negatively and was thinking more problems ahead and was getting very fearful of everything. Dolly was very encouraging under the circumstances. I was getting my asthma attacks almost every day. Stress of making all of these decisions at the same time was making me sick. I was heavily coughing and my breathing was totally unstable. I was worried and nervous about everything happening around me. Dolly took me a private military doctor in Jullundur Kent on the suggestion of a pharmacist. The doctor told me to join the job at the new location and explained me that there was no reason for you to stay idle and let anxiety take over you. Dolly also suggested me to go to this new location Fridabad near New Delhi.

I went to my new location and joined my job and took over the charge of my new office and stores. In about couple of weeks I got my new government provided residence and Dolly and my daughters Komal and Dipika joined me over there. I was still consumed with my problems and I was trying to resolve the requirement of my loan agreement. I had no money to pay off my debts. I found out from my friend Dev that Mr. Sangha in USA offers loan to engineers coming to USA.I wrote to Mr. Sangha asking if he could loan me money to come to USA. He exactly knew what embassy requirements were and agreed to loan me any amount I needed as he knew that I already had an USA immigrant visa. He agreed to loan me six hundred dollars as draft I was supposed to bring with me to fulfill my visa requirement and he also agreed to advance me more money to take care of my financial problems with my study loan etc. It was about first week of February just about when Dipika was only about one month old. I had not even spend any time playing with my new baby daughter. She was not yet used to me. Whenever I would pick her in my arms, she would want to go to her mom. I would look her face which would tell me," Go Dad, Go to USA. We shall all be fine and join you there". Like she knew what was going on with me exactly. Yet these was my own thoughts and dreams which were being reflected through her existence my own courage was playing havoc with me. One moment I felt positive and next moment I was worried and anxious.

In the last week of February 29, 1971, I got a letter from USA which was from Mr. Sangha. He agreed to loan me as much money I wanted on the condition that I would pay him back about two and a half time the amount in dollars. I took that letter and read that again and again. I was being bombarded by positive and negative thoughts about my future in USA. One moment I thought," What happens if I don't get a job in USA and a suitable job soon? Who will take care of my two daughters and wife until I get them there in USA?" Finally after deep thinking and some sleepless nights I decided to leave India. My life was already torn upside down. I thought what else could be there. But I also believed in that if you continue struggling long enough to achieve anything in life in spite of setbacks or failures God shall help you to create whatever you want to create or change in your own life. The main thing is to keep pursuing and continue your efforts honestly and long enough to achieve success or accomplishing your own desire or ambition. The road to success is always rough and long but being persistent and hard work always bring out the results a person wants and that is why I believe in the philosophy that we are the creator of our own destiny and our own Karma and that will take us whichever direction we want to go.

Thinking about the circumstantial practicality at that time, all my households were lying in Amritsar. I was in Fridabad about eight-nine hours away. It was night time. Komal and

Dipika had gone to sleep next to their mom and me on a queen size bed. We always liked to keep them close to us all the time. While they were both sleeping comfortably in our bed we picked them and moved them to their bed so that they keep sleeping.

That night Dolly told me," You should go to USA and do not worry about us. We would all survive one way or the other." She was very strong in her statements and I saw a very brave woman in her. I was always timid in making decisions but she made it for me and took away all my worries and anxieties.

Around first March 1, 1971, I took out the letter from Mr. Sangha of USA and took a train to Patiala at night. It was about eight hour's journey by train to my home where my parents and my younger sister lived. I reached there in the morning. I met my mom and dad and my younger sister for about couple of hours. I ate food my mom made for me. I was leaving for bus stand to catch a bus to Sangrur. My dad said he would see me off at the bus station. Perhaps he wanted to know what was going on with me. While we both were on way to bus stand on foot we talked and I told him about my loan situation and the letters I received from college and also told him about my visit to college and what I was told that my oldest brother Sushi reported about my leaving the country without paying my loan.

I told my dad that the purpose of my trip to a small village close to Sangrur was to borrow money from Sangha's family so that I could pay off my student loan. I also told him that I had already arranged to buy my air ticket from fly now and pay later scheme offered by Swissair those days. He was my dad who was very much concerned about me and my welfare. He asked me," Son, how would you pay that much money which you are borrowing from Sangha's family ". I said," Dad, don't worry. God would help me with your blessings. My little girl especially Dipika would help me as she would want to come to me. I believe. "She is born to send me to USA and would always be my inspiration". In our continued conversation I asked dad if he would keep Dolly, Dipika and Komal with him in house until the time I would get them there in USA to join me. I told him that I would send him money to take care of them as soon as I get the job in USA. I would send you money even after they all join me there for taking care of them also, and I would be waiting for them in USA.

He said," This is their home too. I shall be proud that they would stay with us". I said as soon as I got the job I would get them over there as it would be hard for me too to stay alone without them and I would send you money. He said," Go ahead son, I am with you. If god has planned for you and children to go to USA and grow over there, I am sure that would happen and I would be glad that you chased your destiny where ever it lies and I am sure wherever in world you live you shall be our son.".

We had reached the bus stand and the bus had arrived. I took the bus. My dad waved me well by and was walking away from bus. My dad was still in a very fair health. He never gained or lost weight so far as I knew. He was dressed very leisurely. As the bus was accelerating I looked back through bus window. He seemed lost in our recent conversation as I dropped lot of load on him in a short time.

After about an hour and a half, bus reached Sangrur. I had to take another bus for about fifteen minutes more to reach a drop bus stand for a village. After the bus dropped me at this stop I walked about half mile to reach the village and the house I was supposed to go. This was Sangha's house in Panjab in district of Sangrur. A young man who was the bother in law of Mr. Sangha USA came out of that house and greeted me. I told him that I had come to get money. He said. "I already knew that you were coming. Just wait here in this room for about ten minutes and I would bring the money from the bank."

I waited about twenty minutes. He came back with money on his motor cycle. It was about 11:00 AM of Monday morning. I got the money which he gave me and he told me that all the papers had been signed by me under the loan agreement. I received the money and started my journey to Bus Stand on foot with money stored in my brief case which were lot of money to walk with those days_-----.

Reaching the bus stand I took bus to Sangrur. From Sangrur I took a bus straight to Chandigarh and I could reach to My Panjab Engineering College about fifteen minutes before closing. I handed over the total amount of my loan to the loan clerk and asked him to write a receipt. He wrote me a receipt and was gracious enough to write me a clearance letter that I had paid my loan in full under the agreement and prior to date I was expected to pay. It was about 5:30 PM in the evening. Timing was very crucial. I went straight to railway station Chandigarh to catch a train back to Ballabgarh.

It was about eight hours in train from Chandigarh to Ballabgarh. It had been about 24 hours since I had been sitting in train or in bus in India and under great anxiety and nervousness. Every moment I was thinking what would happen next, in case I missed the person or office personnel to finish my task.

Tuesday morning, about 11:00 AM I reached Ballabgarh after travelling about eight hours in train and two hours in a bus from Delhi to Ballabgarh. Daljit was waiting for me and was getting her nerves strained about what was happening around her. She was worried if everything would happen as planned and weather I would be able to go to USA.

Before I left Panjab Engineering College, Chandigarh, the loan clerk before giving me clearance warned me that some previous letters written to passport office and to the airports about me might stand in your way and suggested to show his written clearance letter and certificate if asked at the airport. I had no confidence that the way the system in India, I would be able to leave for USA.

It was already 5:00PM. I walked out of the loan office of engineering college. On my way back, I was feeling why I was treated like a criminal. I was not planning to run away from my obligations. I even continued paying my insurance premium from USA and that was life Insurance corporation of India which never responded even my letters about my life insurance policy. India is still plagued with poor customer service and corruption at all levels still prevails and no hope of any change.

I took a bus to Railway Station Chandigarh. I knew that a train went to Delhi every night at about 11: PM and I was planning to catch that train. The bus reached the railway station and I could catch the train and took a seat in the compartment. I was sitting in the train and was feeling totally drained out of all the energy had not slept for about fifty six hours in a stretch. I had been travelling continuously either in bus or in train and I was closing my eyes in my seat. Next to me an old lady noticed my discomfort and offered me more room from her seat so that I could sleep. I thanked her and tried to go back to sleep. But I was so tired and drained and was wide awake and looked over every railway station where the train stopped. Next morning around 7:00AM I reached Delhi. I walked over to the bus station which was just a few hundred yards from the railway station. I caught the bus going to Ballabgarh.

I reached Ballabgarh about 11:00 AM and went straight to my office. I took care of some office essentials and important messages and worked in the office which was such like going through my official mail and responding to some urgent messages. I also sent a message to my wife Baljit telling her that I was back. After I worked about couple of hours I went to my Kothi(residence at electric substation). Baljit asked me how everything went. I told her that I was hungry and need food and energy to talk to her. She gave me my afternoon supper/dinner. After eating my food I went to sleep in my bed. It was very early in the evening and Baljit was still talking to me and was very anxious to know about my trip and I said," I shall let you know everything in the morning". She said," This is only 5:30 PM and you are going to sleep". I said," I know. I kissed goodnight to Dipika, Komal and Baljit and went to sleep."

Next morning, I looked up the date on my visa letter. The expiry date of my visa was March 12, 1971. It was March 6th that day. I called my travel agent in Chandigarh to arrange my flight on March 10, 1971. He called me back that my travel ticket had been booked for a flight on March 10th,at 3:00 PM through Indian Air Lines from Delhi to Bombay and my departure from Bombay was at 4:00 AM on March 11,1971 and arrival in New York same day which was just a day before my visa expire.

I had no more time to plan or do anything except making my luggage and brief case ready. Next morning, I went to my office and called my executive engineer in Delhi who was my immediate supervisor and requested her for a four day leave of absence. He agreed and approved my four day leave and off time based on my family hardship. It was March 7, 1971. One of my colleague invited us for a dinner at their residence. He happened to be a Muslim as India had a great population of Muslims. His wife made special food for us which was not" Halal". While we were enjoying our dinner, he told us very truthfully that he got a call from Amritsar that day and the person said," I saw Mr Vatas last month buying luggage which was suite cases. My guess is he is leaving the country as he was buying luggage which only people buy to go to a foreign and overseas country. "I told him clearly that I did buy such luggage but rest I had no idea as I myself was not confident of leaving the country yet".

I was still in doubt for all my arrangements. I was thinking," What if my clearance certificate did not make to the right departments and my passport might get cancelled and I might get stopped at the airport. My department never cleared me for going overseas and Govt. of India might stop me for leaving the country without permission. My loan office at engineering college might not send the clearance letter to passport office. My passport might had already been cancelled". I thanked my friend for the great dinner and left. I wanted to talk to him more and disclose my plans but my lack of confidence and fear in my self-stopped me in doing so. Baljit asked me why I did not tell him that I was leaving. I said," I was not sure whether I would be able to go or not. Authorities might stop me at the airport for any reason like I had no clearance from my Panjab State Electricity Board or the information about that I had paid my loan might not be circulated to passport office and other departments". I was thinking positive at one moment and negative at next moment.

Same evening Of March 7th, 1971. Dolly shouted that Dipika wanted to come to you as she (Dolly) wanted to do her cooking for dinner. I grabbed Dipika from her and embraced her. She was only two months old baby, I took her in my lap and looked at her. She could not express positivity or negativity of her feelings. Her face was full of smiles and free of our any worry. I asked her if I should go to USA or not. Her smiles and fearless way had me decided what I should do under such circumstances. Her vibes were very positive and encouraging to me. I am really proud of her that she did not only motivate me to go to USA and immigrate but also she became a very successful and an honest immigrant lawyer after her own struggles with financial situation in the process. Actually she made me decide what should I do under such circumstances and her positive vibes made me strong to do and decide things I was thinking and trying deciding and was postponing. Finally I picked up the phone and called my executive engineer and who was my immediate supervisor and we had never met each other. I asked him for a four day leave of absence on account of family hardship which was nothing except of my own social situation and the future of my own children. He agreed and granted me four day of vacation and time off. It was about 7:00PM in the evening.

I called one of my senior Line Superintendent and my store keeper along with my sub divisional clerk who handled all my office cash transactions and administrative work. They all lived in the same colony and were ready to come to office in any emergency. I told them, "I have to give charge of my responsibility to senior line superintendent and handover my keys of cash chest as well as all the stores to him after counting all the money in the chest". All the handing over and taking over was performed as per established government rules and practices. I shook hand with everyone in my room and walked back to my kothi residence.

Baljit already had started making my luggage ready and said we would all be leaving for Modinagar early in the morning.

Next morning which was eighth March, 1971, we all woke up early. Even Dipika and Komal were up and wide awake. They were small children. Dipika was only two months old and Komal was less than two years old. We all were at the bus stand at about 9:00AM and could get bus to Delhi and second bus to Modinagar which was only forty minutes bus ride. We made to Modinagar at about 12:30 PM. This was the place my sister in law Nimmil was from. We met all the family. They were all very happy to see us all. That night we spent with them.

Dolly told me that I would do my best to make up with your parents and would give them same regard and love which I gave to my own parents. She was very truthful in her statements which she always have proved and I always believed her 100% as I have felt her to be like that all the time. I always knew that my beliefs and aspirations may or may or be the reality of life. I always doubted my own self for whatever I achieved but I stayed persistent and continued hoping for the best to happen. Dal went to live with my parents. She is very outspoken and sincere for all my family members and would do whatever was best for them under all circumstances. But she was a little skeptical about everything. She was not believing in her own self in spite of being very brave.

Next day it was March 9, 1971. It was our anniversary day. Baljit and I decided that we should leave tomorrow afternoon and check into a hotel for our anniversary night. Next day, we left Modinagar after lunch. Everyone wanted to see me off at Airport and planned to see me at the airport on 10th March, 1971.They were all my brother in laws as they were my sister in laws (Urmi)

Real brothers and very loving and affectionate family, and I felt all of them to be my own. It was not easy for me to leave the love of my life as well as my babies Komal and Dipika on the same day when we married and was our anniversary day. I had to leave India the day of my own anniversary.

Baljit and I decided to check in a hotel along with Dipika and Komal at about 4:00PM on 9th March which was our anniversary day and was not known to anyone except us. We took a two bed room where Dolly made Dipika and Komal comfortable on one bed. She told me to go to market down stair and buy something to eat for our dinners. I went down and looked around. The hotel was only on the second floor and first floor was all kinds of shops and restaurants which was typical for Delhi bazars and markets. I went to a carry out restaurant and bought some Poories (fried Chapattis) and chick peas for us to eat as our dinner. We all ate the food except Madhu who was still only two months old and was still on Jit's breast milk only.

After travelling in a bus and Rikshas we were all exhausted. At about 8:00PM, Komal and Dipika went to sleep on their bed. I was looking at both of them and was thinking that I would not see my babies for some time. But in my mind, I was determined that I would bring them to USA with me as soon as I could.

Jiti was looking at me and part of her was thinking ahead and somewhat nervous, "What we three will do without you and who would take care of us?" On the other hand I myself was totally consumed thinking weather I would be able to depart for USA without any problem. Under a very stressful situation we made love on our anniversary. I was very unsure about leaving my country, family, parents and many dear friends and near relatives behind. Jiti was more optimistic and said," I am sure you will be ok and you will get us all over there in USA at your earliest possible and our little family will be together again". But I was very realistic about and knew that I was jumping into an unknown territory. I told her that in case I could not adjust myself in America, I would see you back soon. Please give me at least six months and would send some money as soon as I got any job.

Sam! Your Nanni is a brave woman. She belongs to a family of fair and honest peoples based upon my interaction with some of her family members but they were like rest of the society were confirmed to prevailing social taboos and restrictions. Later in my contact and study of their family I found out that the famous independence fighter and martyr Sardar Udam Singh of Sunam was her grand uncle who has been mentioned in history of India and especially of Panjab as a freedom fighter in India's struggle for independence from British rule.

She told me," Go Kishi, may be our luck lies in USA and not in India. May be our daughters are supposed to grow up in a different world, I shall survive and keep my daughters safe in your parent's house until you get us all with you in USA". Next day it was 10th March of 1971. We all woke up later than usual and this was Dipika who woke first and she woke all of us as she wanted her feed. It was about 9:00AM. I went down stair in the market and brought two cups of tea, one for myself and the other for Jiti. We both took our tea. Komal was hungry too as she woke up and wanted something to eat. At about 10:00AM I went down again in the market and brought some food to eat from small restaurants close by. It was about the same food which we ate night before but from some different restaurant (fried Chapaties called Poories and Chhollas called chick peas) and some milk for Komal. BalJit made us all eat and made us ready by 1:00 PM. She fed Dipika also. We were all ready to leave for airport and I checked out from the hotel and hired a taxi to New Delhi airport which is now called Indira Gandhi International airport of Delhi.It was about 2:30 PM and we were all at the airport. My brother in laws from Modinagar reached in time to see me off and they were all young and were very excited to send me off to USA. I only remembered their youthful faces and their energetic ways of doing things. My flight time was about 3:30 PM. BalJit gave me 150 rupees and asked me to get foreign exchange of eight dollars which was allowed those days for travelers to US. She had no idea of the exchange rate and gave me more money than what I needed for eight dollars.

I exchanged for eight dollars with about ninety eight rupees and I was left about fifty two rupees with me. But the airport rules were such that I could not go back and hand over the excess fifty two rupees I had to my family. But it was ok as it probably was for public safety. Earlier my friend brought some eatable burfi (An Indian Sweet made out of sugar and milk). He gave me before I entered the airport and was disallowed by the airport official saying foods are not allowed on flights. I left there and gave back to my friend Dev. But he had a knowledge of system and he gave some money to the official and he brought himself and handed over to me that box of sweets. But I was not allowed to go back to my family to handover some fifty two rupees back to my family who needed the money. On the other hand I was thinking if made an issue official might cancel my right to travel outside the country without any reasons. I was afraid that I was never given any no objection by BMB (Bhakra Management Board) from the government job I was holding in BMB to leave for USA my loan clearance papers might not had reached Passport Officer.

Under these circumstances, I handed over my luggage to Swiss Air representative. I was thinking that just to get eight dollars' worth of exchange from the exchange counter I was not allowed to go back to say good bye to my family, friends and relatives. It was not all the fault of the system only but I myself was so nervous and fearful that I could not dare to look back towards my family and friends who came to see me off due to the way old airport was structured. In my own mind and heart, I remembered every moment and every face who came to wish me farewell on the airport as I was very much attached with every one of them. It was hard for me to leave every one and the country I was born in. I was simply looking for a new future and a country to live in and wanted my children to grow in a free land and full of opportunities.

At the same time when I was leaving India, what your Nanni was going through was very dramatic situation in her own life which she never experienced before as she had no money to go back to home and pay for taxi, she felt as if she had lost everything but was holding her two daughters closely, older was your mom Ryan and younger one was your Auntie Dipika.

After we all visited our parents' home in Patiala, my dad agreed that all of you guys (Dolly, Komal and Dipika) can stay with him during this time of transition and I told him that I would be sending money for them as soon as I get a job in USA. My dad agreed and accepted them to live with him as she had already got attached to his granddaughters. Dal also got ready to take care my old parents in the stage they were both in which was just old age and also my younger sister who was still unmarried.

It was about 3:30 PM, almost my Indian Air Lines flight departure. I had to go in a bus which took us to the plane which was about a mile away on the run away waiting for passengers to board. This was my first ever flight in airplane from Delhi to Bombay (Now Mumbai).This was only two hour flight. I enjoyed the flight and the refreshments the airline served in the plane. I was worried how much I had to pay them for the food as my travel agent or no one else never told me that the foods served were included in the air fare. I was surprised that no one asked me to pay for the food. I reached Mumbai airport at about 5:45 PM.

The airhostess of Swissair received me at the air gate. I was not expecting that but they were wonderful and very much helping. She told me that my next flight depart time was at 4:00 AM in the morning. She asked me if I would like to check in Hotel and come back early in morning at about 3:00AM. I said that would be fine. She arranged a taxi to and back from the Hotel and had me stay at Taj Mahal. My luggage was already checked in to New York. I along with my briefcase in my hand took a taxi cab to Taj Mahal hotel. On my way to Hotel I looked back into my wallet found those fifty two dollars which BalJit gave me through her normal generosity and I was not planning to take out of the country this Indian currency under the laws. I asked the Taxi Driver if he could take me to a drug store or a pharmacy shop. He said, "Yes. Actually it is right on our way and I do not have to drive any extra". He was kind enough to stop at a pharmacy shop. I asked the pharmacist if I could buy some of my Asthma medicines from you and I did not have any prescription with me but I had been prescribed to take and gave him the name of the pills I was on. He said," Ye I have these pills and how many you want? "I Said," Give me whatever number you can sell me for forty five rupees (About a dollar in today's exchange rate). He gave me about six month consumption of my prescribed asthma medicine pills. I felt great thinking about that I had enough medicines to survive for at least six months.

The Taxi reached the Hotel and I checked in. It was about 8:00 PM.I ate my dinner at the Hotel Restaurant and went to my room to sleep and relax. I was worried about getting up early too and requested the hotel receptionist to give me a wakeup call at about 2:00 AM.I lied down in my bed in hotel room very anxious to get up at 2:00 AM. I was not able to sleep fully and almost rested in my bed for a few hours and woke up myself at about 2:00 AM. While I was already awake I got a wakeup call ring from the hotel desk. I got up and shaved and took shower and was ready down stairs waiting for taxi. Exactly around 3:00AM, the same taxi driver came to pick me and drop me at the airport. I grabbed my brief case which had my visa and passport papers and got into the taxi. In about fifteen minutes, we were at the airport and dropped me at the Swissair departures counter. I gave him two rupees tip and he was very happy and thankful. He even wished me good luck in America.

The Swissair hostess checked me in the flight and in the checkout terminal. I noticed at the terminal there was a big written sign again that it was illegal to take Indian Currency out of the country. I looked again in my wallet. There was a five rupee note and some change in my pocket. Walking in the airport, I felt thirsty. I asked a waiter if he could get me a coke. He brought a tall glass of coke for me. I asked him, "How much I owe you". He said," Seventy five Paisa's". I opened my wallet and found exactly same amount of change in it. I gave him the exact change for the coke and before he could leave I gave him the five rupee note and told him that was your Tip. He said," It is too much, Sir. I do not make that much in two weeks". He was very happy and said," God will bless with good luck".

At about 4:00AM a bus took all the passengers for boarding to Swissair plane waiting on the run way. I got my seat in the plane and took off for USA. I was relieved off all the anxiety and my doubts as soon as the plane was in air. Although I had read about technology a lot during my education years yet I had not seen its application to human life. In spite of being an electrical engineer, my knowledge of outside India was very limited.

My first stop after I departed from Mumbai was Zurich. I had about six hour layover at that airport. As soon as I reached Zurich, I got down from the airplane and a Swissair hostess explained to me that I would be at the airport for about six hours and mine next flight would be later in the evening and from gate number seven. In my own mind I was still thanking God for letting me leave India without any problem and I knew that I was breathing normally during my flight.

At the Zurich airport, looking at some signs I found and entered a restroom. I had never seen that much cleanliness in the restroom as compared to what I had seen in India and what I was used too. I used the toilet and was looking for the way to flush it. It was different than what I was using in India. There was no chain to pull. I looked over the whole wall of the rest room. I touched and tried every shining steel fixtures to flush. But as soon as I touched, there was an announcement on the airport," Mr. Vatas, a passenger from Bombay to New York. Please report to Swissair counter". Immediately I thought," Did I touch some wrong pipe for flushing the toilet or my Government of India employer or Indian passport office had caught up with me and about some problem. In a rush I came out of the rest rooms. As soon as I came out of the restrooms, almost right in the exit doors, there was a Swissair hostess was waiting for me to come out. She might have noticed me entering the rest rooms. I was wearing a black suit and a tie. She asked me very nicely," Are you Mr. Vatas travelling to New York?" I was almost trembling in my pants. I said," Yes Madame." She said," I have reserved a room for you at the airport hotel. You can go this way and follow the sign to reach there. You can check in there and sleep or relax for a few hours. You will also be served the meals if so desired". I took a long breath and thanked God for not being in a situation what I thought I was in. I followed the sign and reached at the airport hotel. I checked in and went to my room.

It was a bright sunny day. I could not sleep or even relax. I was excited to see where I was. I had been travelling continuously every day for the whole last week. I was alert and wide awake.

A waitress knocked my room and brought luncheon menu to me. I picked the vegetarian menu and she brought my lunch pretty fast. I ate my lunch of eggs, toast and some boiled vegetables. Immediately after I finished my lunch, I got a call from airline the voice on the line said," Please report to the departing gate within 30 minutes". I picked up my brief case and started walking towards the departing gate. Upon arriving at the gate, I was seated in the plane as I was the last passenger to board.

Sam, I am going to stop for a few minutes about "My Story" and talk to you about your Nanni. She had a laser surgery as her tear glands were closed. I took her to the hospital and she had a successful surgery on her left eye. Next week she would be having her right eye operated. She is in good spirits. Ryan, you know she loves eating from her own hand which means to me that she believed in working for her food. She is a hard worker and very caring to others. She is great and I love her the way she is. She is very independent woman. Ryan smiled and opened his mouth to say," I love her too".

Let us go back to my story. My flight took off for New York. I got the window seat. Right next to me a Jewish busyness man from Bombay came and took the seat. Very nice guy and he introduced himself to me and we were talking as if we knew each other before. He asked me if I had been to USA before. I told him that I had never been to USA and this was my first trip. He said," I have been to USA several time on my business trips". Just at the same moment the air hostess interrupted our conversation and said," Swissair is serving dinner on flight and asked if we want to order any drink". We both ordered beer. She brought the beer and asked for fifty cents. I gave her a dollar and she gave me some francs which I never knew anyway what type of currency that was. She gave me some coins which I never seen before. She asked me what kind of food I want Vegetarian or Non Vegetarian meal? I happened to say," Non vegetarian as I ate eggs, chicken and mutton in India. I had no idea of other meats to eat". She brought for me a Non-Vegetarian dinner. I ate whatever she brought but had no idea what she served.

In about eight or nine hours, the flight reached JFK Air Port of New York. I came out of the airplane and the airhostess guided us to immigration. I gave my envelope of Immigration Visa which was marked," DO NOT OPEN. ONLY IMMIGERATION OFFICIAL SHOULD OPEN THIS ENVELOPE". The officer I handed over my Visa opened in front of me and in a few minutes he printed or just gave me a permanent immigration visa card. I was very surprised how fast he gave me the card and asked me to collect my baggage and proceed to your airline counter. I came back to the baggage area and saw my baggage going again and again on the belt conveyor. I had no idea what TO DO. No one else baggage was on the belt except mine. I did not see any one removing their baggage. I could not figure out why only my suitcases were on the belt going around and around. I was happy to see my luggage and started waiting the belt conveyer to stop before I remove my luggage. I had no idea about the rules or the norms. I had come from a country where the luggage was being handled by coolies and there were no belt conveyers or baggage handlers. As I was still thinking at that moment whether I should pick my luggage from the running belt or not, a Swissair official tapped my shoulder. He said, "Sir, Is that your baggage?" I said, "Yes". He said," You can pick your luggage and bring to our counter and I shall book it to your destination".

I took my two suitcases from the belt conveyer and took that to Swissair counter. The airhostess booked my baggage to Cincinnati airport and she told me that your next flight leaves from La Guardia airport and you had a helicopter flight to La Guardia. She pointed towards a helicopter ready to take off and a door to reach that and said," Go straight to that door and catch that helicopter flight". To me it was a big glass wall and a door which I never saw before. I walked towards that glass wall and looking for a door and came back disappointed as I did not see any door. I told that Swissair lady," Madame, I could not find any door over there. She smiled and said, "OK I shall take you there". She walked with me towards the door and explained that the door was an automatic and only opens when you get close. Just see how it happens. As we both were close by that time the door opened. I thanked her and she wished me good luck. I walked towards the waiting helicopter in the open. It was raining and it was cold for me. It was the month of March in New York. I boarded the helicopter first time in my life and so were my yesterday's airplane flights.

As the helicopter flew very low, I was looking towards the tall buildings and the many multi story buildings in New York. I was very excited to see the sky line of New York. I was very interesting to see my new country of USA and more over I was feeling great as I was legally in USA and on a permanent resident visa. One minute I would think about not to worry about my past problems and start as a fresh time in my life, on the other minute, I would be anxious and worry about where I would live in Cincinnati.

In about twenty minute, the helicopter landed at the LaGuardia airport. I checked in at TWA airline counter and took flight to Cincinnati. The flight was coming through Petersburg PA and there was a stop at the airport. The plane landed at this airport I could not understand any announcement and thought I was in Cincinnati. I asked the gentleman sitting next to me," Is this Cincinnati? My way of pouncing Cincinnati was like "Kinkinnati" as I read cat as a Kat. The gentleman was very nice and understood that I was very new to the country. He told me the right pronunciation of the name of Cincinnati and he also told me that that stop was for Petersburg and your s would be next stop. I stayed in the plane the gentleman shook my hand and left the plane. Petersburg was his destination. I still remember his face and his kindness as he taught me how to pronounce the name of city of Cincinnati.

At my next stop I reached my destination of Cincinnati airport. It was about 8:30 PM. Now I had already learned how to grab luggage from a running baggage belt conveyor. I collected my luggage and started following signs and reached ground transportation area. I reached my briefcase to find the paper where Mr. Gill's information was. I found his phone number and reached the telephone to call him. The telephone was hanging on a wall. But the telephone did not look like what I had in my office. In India I was having a dial which would rotate when I dialed a phone number kind of a rotary dial phone. The phone on the airport was a numerical pad which I had no idea that existed. It was pay phone and was asking me drop a quarter. I was puzzled and confused and it was already dark. I was wondering if I would have to sleep on the airport and try next morning to dial the number correctly. I had no idea how a quarter looked like, the change I had was either dollar or some coins which were given to me on flight.

A gentleman noticed me struggling with phone to make a call. He came and asked me if he could help me. Back in India no one ask you to help even if you need help. There the way I heard those days in India that those who would come forward to help you would rob or pick pocket you. I was very skeptical but the guy looked very trustworthy and was very serious to help me. I requested him if he could dial the phone number for me as I did not know how to dial the phone which was digital. I took all my change and showed him and asked if he could pick a quarter. He looked over my coins and noticed the coins were from either Swiss or European exchange coins. He said," It is OK, I have a quarter. He put his own quarter in the phone slot and dialed the phone number I gave him". The voice answered on the other end as Mr. Sangha. I wanted to pay the gentleman his quarter but as I looked he was ready to go. I thanked him before he left and tried to give a dollar bill which I had. He was very generous and did not take any money from me and left. He also said," Good Luck".

On my phone conversation with Mr. Sanghal, I requested him to pick me from the airport. Unfortunately Mr. Gill had gone through a tragic family happening. His wife gave birth to a son who was paralyzed from waist down as detected by doctors at the time of child birth.

Sam! You were not born like this. You were born normal and had no problems or any abnormal health disability. Ryan smiled simply hearing his name. I said," SAM you are very good and everyone loves you." SAM smiled again. I was also very much gratified to see him smiling and happy.

Going back to my journey, Mr. Sangha asked me if I could take a taxi to his home and explained his family situation. I was also lost. I had no idea how or which way to ask or explain to taxi driver. I requested again and asked Mr. Sangha to come and pick me from the airport as I was almost feeling lost. He agreed and came in his car to pick me after about an hour, He agreed and told me that he was coming. His house was about forty five miles from airport. Around 10:30 PM, we reached Mr. Sangha's house which was in a suburb of Cincinnati.

Mr. Sangha's sister in law served us late dinner and she was awake and talking to me till 1:30 AM about life in USA. She was very attractive and honest looking woman. Mr. Sangha also gave some orientation of employment condition in the United States and particularly in Ohio. He told me lot of peoples are looking for jobs. He gave a copy of his own resume as a sample to guide me to prepare for my own resume and asked me to get it typed. He made me aware of the situation that boys who came through him were still looking for a job. I was very tired and my sleep timing was all messed up due to Jet lag and time difference in the two continents. I was hosted a small guest bed room and I was so tired that I went to bed very fast.

Next morning I woke up and Mr. Sangha's sister in law talked to me some of the things in USA. I also talked to Mrs. Sangha and saw her new baby and talked to her about her about the little boy. The baby looked very cute. I felt for that cute boy and had no idea whom to blame for the sufferings he was going through. Actually that is one reason we all believe in GOD or Nature which produced us all. But there is nothing you can say or explain to these little ones why and how it all happened all this for them At around 10:00AM, we all ate breakfast. Under my contract with Mr. Sangha He was supposed to keep me for four days, but after I found how much he was busy and stressed, I called my friend Dev S who told me that he was on way to pick me up from Sangha's residence. At about 11:00AM, I wished farewell and thanked Mr. Gill for his financial support and other things he did for me like picking me from airport and keeping me overnight at his place. Although all these things were part of his contract with me yet he performed under his tough situation. As soon as Dev arrived I loaded my two suit case in his car and we both left. Dev brought me to his apartment in down town apartment where there were two more boys were living with him. One of them Tony I knew back from India as my close colleague's son as he came with Dev also. Another one called Ambi who was also from Panjab and I met him first time and a great wonderful and truthful guy. The apartment was very big with four bedrooms. They gave me a bedroom. Everyone was still unemployed and looking for a suitable job as they were all engineers. Dev, Tony and Amby came about 3to 4 months earlier but all of them were still looking for a job. Next day Tony and Dev took me to an Indian girl Ramani who was a student in university of Cincinnati. She knew how to type. I asked her if she could type my resume. She gladly helped me and typed my two page resume the same day.

My thoughts had been interrupted Sam! I got a bad news. I just learned that my older brother Parkash had passed away. I had talked and written about him earlier in my story. I was shocked to know and had no shoulder to cry on. My thoughts and prayers were with my niece who was born over hear in USA and my sister in law. They had no one around them to take care. Last year I saw them all happy during my visit. I do understand that death is the way God recycle life for our betterment. But the death always leave an impact on peoples it touches. I and my brother Parkash had a long time together before and after we both had families. He got a heart attack. It happened around 2nd or third June, 2012.

I know I was the one who made a decision in the family to immigrate to USA. Only time I really missed India was when someone close to me died. I was so far away that I could never be there and I had to take control of my feelings myself. I was not in India when my father died, my mother died and my brothers died. Only thing I could say that I loved them the way they were and would not change a thing about them if I had to live again with them and apologize for not being there at their last time. But I am happy that my children and my nephews and nieces (Theni, Manu and, Sue, Anile and Deep) had opportunities which they could not have in India. I have no idea how they feel about being isolated from so many relatives. But they all are happy and settled which gives me immense happiness too. Sam, your Auntie Theni is married to Dr. Gupta and has your cousin Nate as their son, Your Auntie Manu is married to your uncle Chuck and your Auntie Sue is married to your uncle Josh and has your cousins John, Mina, Nina and Bobby.

Let us go back to my story in 1971 when I came to USA and started looking for a job and was very anxious to get one as soon as I could. The un-employment rate was very high at that time. The girl who typed my resume was,' Raminick'. She typed my two page resume and she was a student in UC. This all happened in the first week of my coming to USA. All my friends said," Relax, we have been over hear longer than you, which I knew was just two or three months at the most. It will take some time to get a job in this country, unless you want to work on a car wash down stair. They will pay $ 2.50/hr." They told me that they brought six hundred dollars when we came and we are still spending and living on that. Whenever our that money would be over we would go down stair and start working on that car wash. The day we would have no money left for eating we would go to this car wash or some another minimum wage job. I said," I left my two precious daughters and my wife in India and they had no money and no one's support. I want to bring them over here as soon as I can". All these friends I was talking to were UN-Married (Singles)and had no idea what I was talking about and what I had been going through when I hit the bed every night. How it is to be in a situation where your family is plain suffering. Although they were all with my parents yet who would pay for their living and lodging and the children needs. They had no idea how I got married and what were my problems in addition to being married. I was very much concerned about the welfare of my daughters and my wife and I always every moment missed them as they were love of my life and they were all simply part of me left behind in India while I was in USA.

In about second week of me in USA, I and my friends decided to visit one of my friends who came earlier than me and he lived in Middletown, Ohio. On Saturday, we all decided to go and visit him. It was a rainy day. Middletown is about forty five minutes' drive from Cincinnati. That day it was raining hard and was very cloudy and dark. We drove by city of Middletown building in down town and I spotted a sign for city of engineering department. I requested my friends to drop me there but everybody was against dropping me in the rain and were not thinking the way I was thinking. They said," You are crazy. Whom do you think you will see this raining day and on a Saturday? Everything is supposed to be closed". We all went to our friend's house in Middletown. He served us all with tea and all my friends started to talk to each other. I slipped out when they were all talking. I sneaked out of his apartment and started walking in rain towards the city building which was in down town. It was still drizzling like a drizzle rain. I was wearing a black suit which I bought from India. I walked out and walked about 2/3 of blocks which took me to city of Middletown building. I entered the building through main door. There was no one around. I was still trying to find my way to engineering department of city of Lebanon. A voice came from the dark corridor of the building," May I help you?"

I walked slowly towards this voice and found a gentleman with jean's and bunch of keys hanging on his jeans and blue shirt with his name on him. He wore glasses. I told him that I was looking for an engineering job in your engineering department. He said," Follow me. Today the offices are closed". After opening couple of doors, he opened his office door. It was a big office. Before I could sit he gave me a job application which I filled out completely. I had no resume with me which I wanted to attach with my application. I handed over that application to him and told him that I would be able to bring my resume later on. Just standing next to me he glanced over my application and noticed my qualification and credentials as listed in the application. He asked me to come in to his big office. I could feel that he was a big boss simply looking his big office. But I never knew and thought who he could be. He asked me to have a seat while he was still standing himself. As I was going to sit in the chair he asked me to have he introduced himself as a city manager of the city. He told me that he was interested in hiring me. He had already looked over what I filled in the form. He chatted with me just a few minutes and asked me if I could come Monday for a second interview which would be official. I said," Yes Sir!" He also asked me to bring my resume along. I went to see him in his office on Monday and as required I also took my resume with me. He asked his city divisional superintendent for electric to give me a tour of the generating plant and the city distribution system. After showing the city electrical system, I was offered a job and was given couple of days to accept the offer officially.

I came out of the city building and walked very happily to parking lot where my friends were waiting for me in the car. I told my friends the news that I had been offered a job and I had two days to decide. My friends were so annoyed and asked me why I did not accept the offer then and there and told me that I was just a fool not to accept the offer. Back in my heart I knew that they were right, but I postponed the acceptance just to make the city believe that I made a well thought decision after a day later. Actually I myself was impatient to get to work and to earn money to send to India to support my family in India as well as to get them here in USA with meal my friends were after me again and again and wanted me to explain to them what made me not to accept the offer. None of them knew that sometimes I could not make abrupt decisions and I had no idea whether that was my bad or good quality. But it was always a problem for me. I finally told my friends," OK guys, I shall call him tomorrow".

My friends were very happy and wanted me to buy some beer to celebrate. I told them to stop at the next gas station and I would pick some beer. A few minutes later we all stopped at a gas station and I picked some beer for my friends. Two of my friends in the back seat opened the cans already and started drinking. We were on our way to Cincinnati from Middletown, Ohio. After about fifteen minutes, one of my friend Tony who was sitting in the back said," I do not feel anything and the other friend confirmed the same. We were all very serious and wanted to know the truth. We took the next exit and stopped again on another gas station and asked the gas station attendant why the beer we bought had no buzz and we showed him the empty can. He said," Oh! This is root beer and has no alcohol in it. You guys need something different. He brought some Miller Lite and we bought twelve cans. We were laughing and laughing and that beer started working on all of us.

Next day I called the city manager of Middletown and told him that I accepted his offer and he asked me to join next day and I was at work next day at 8:00 AM as he asked. My city manager was a wonderful person who actually understood my needs and problems and he accommodated me in many ways and helped me in many ways.

My top priority still was to get my Dolly and my two daughters here in USA which was my only inspiration to go through all the discomfort and problems which probably all the immigrants go through. I was going to work every day with that motivation in my mind and wanted to get my family together as soon as I could. I never felt anything in my life beyond except to be with my Baljit and my two little daughters. That was my life and everything I did she was with me and my daughters inspired me and she was in it all the time. Nothing was difficult for me if she was with me and agreed with me in any matter. Some times while sitting alone I wondered how one person's life could affect another person. I was very much dependent on her for lot of things she did for me and at that time she was about ten thousand miles away. She was more charge taking in every situation. In such process she always ignored her own welfare and even her own safety. She was with me in all my decisions and how and where I live even if she was ten thousand miles away from me. My daughters and Dolly always helped me to make

I am very laid back, and she is very aggressive. I shall spend more time in thinking and analyzing while she would just go ahead and start the project and will take charge of it. That probably is a cause that we both complemented each other drawbacks and qualities. Whatever she could do I certainly could not and vice versa. I was always worried about her safety as she does not care when she works in her own kitchen or in his own house doing odd and ends tasks. She gets dedicated to her work and even ignores her own safety many times. She had hurt herself such as burning her self during her cooking in her own kitchen, had cut her legs and scarred her face simply working in her own house and with little things. She had spent weeks in taking care of nuisance wound s many time. She would get into anything and at any place without any proper safety precautions. Her own physical protection is actually nothing as compared to her energy to complete a simple task or a complex job at home. Many time her own dedication to complete a house chore is more than her own comfort or safety.

Sam, just to let you know how I felt when I met your nannie, I was praying every moment to god to help me see her wherever she is. Sometime God made me see her at the time when I was not even expecting or possible. Many times she surprised me and showed up at my home or other locations. My attraction to your nannie was not for her looks or who she was or who were her parents or what was her religion. I am now seventy year old and I am still trying to figure out what attracted me to her. It was like magnets attract positive to negative. That force has not diminished even if I cannot convey her any more. She is a unique individual which god brought into my life for some purpose. You and I would not have been talking if your nannie would not have been a very real person and a beautiful one. She is very sincere and honest and I can rely on her for anything. That was the way I met her first time and that is the way she is even today.

Sam, I was missing your nannie very much when I left her behind about ten thousand miles away in India along with your mom and auntie Dipika. I was praying every day to God to have me and your nannie, mom and your auntie

Dipika. May that was the reason I got the job so fast as compared to my other friends who came to USA even earlier than me.

Your mom, auntie Dipika, and your Nanni spent about nine months with my dad and mom and with my younger sister. She had quite a different experience living in my parents' home. My younger sister was not very comfortable and always tried to sabotage the little stuff. Dal told me that one time she got some milk for your aunti and mom but she took that milk and gave to a dog which was also living in and was part of the family. But your Nanni did not like this as my sister never asked her to use that milk for the dog. But your Nannie had no milk to give to your mom and your auntie but everybody survived in the family except your Nanni who still tell me her story and the amount of anguish she felt about my own sister. But she is a very forgiving person for everyone else except me. If I do something wrong she would never forget and bring the concerns again and again. During her stay with my parents along with your mom and your auntie Dipika my Dad got hurt on his foot as some cabinet which he was working on fell on his foot and his foot got injured badly and he was in a severe pain and were not able to sleep even. My mom asked your Nanni to take care of him and get him treated as she was old and mentally not very sound at that time. Your Nanni sent my Dad in a Riksha and she followed the Riksha and walked herself on foot to an emergency doctor in the market. She got the medical care my dad needed in that situation. He was very happy as soon as he got ok. After a few months his eyes got really in pain and he was not bear the pain in the eyes and was not able to sleep. He woke up your Nanni and told her that he had a severe pain his eyes and hurting and cannot go to sleep. Your Nanni woke up around 1:00 AM and heated some water and added some Boric acid in the water and washed his eyes and gave him some pain pills to sleep. This was the treatment she learned from her older sister who was a registered nurse in hospital. My father could sleep and felt much better the next day. Next day he wrote a letter to me in USA accepting her as her daughter in law and approved that I made a good choice about marrying her he said," She is very dedicated, honest and caring. We could not have found such a girl from the arranged marriage system based on so many social restrictions based upon and on the prevailing caste system". His letter to me was very uplifting and I continued sending him money for their expenditure and for the family. I continued sending money even after Dolly, Komal and Dipika came to USA as I was simply taking care of my own parents. After a little while my dad wrote me that he and my mom were doing OK financially with his pension and along my younger sister and they have enough income from savings to survive and they wanted me to take care of my family over here in USA and he said he would let you know if his economic situation changes due to certain problems. He sincerely wanted me to take care of Dolly, Komal and Dipika over here in USA.

I was so much thinking and consumed in your nannie, mom and your auntie Dipika that I talked to my city manager to help. He told me that he would write anything I wanted to write to Indian Consulate in Delhi to fulfill any condition which is required by Federal laws of immigration. He (The city Manager) wrote a very strong letter to the consulate which was more than the sponsorship letter.

Your Nannie, your mom and your auntie Dipika got the visa to come to USA and join me. This was sometime in November 1971 and I guess it was the first week of November. Two weeks later I received a letter from her that she did receive the visa from the US embassy but she lost that on her way back from embassy. She and your another nannie were travelling in a motor Riksha and when they got down from the Riksha she forgot her small file case at the seat and the visa documents were all in that file case. It all happened the day she received the visa, and she was holding your auntie in her arms and your mom was also by her side along with her other luggage. She was very devastated and was very discouraged as she wrote me. The driver of the motor Riksha had already left and she knew nothing about him and had no information how to find him without his name, address and the organization he was working in a huge city of New Delhi, India.

Your nannie came home at Modinagar totally confused, upset and depressed as she wrote me in her letter. Next day she went back to US Embassy in New Delhi and told her story to the Consulate that she had lost her visa documents. The consular said," What a bad luck! The consular explained her the procedure to have a duplicate visa. She understood many steps she had to take to get a duplicate visa. She went back to my parents in Panjab at Patial. She started working on the procedure to get a duplicate visa such as re applying for different documents which she lost.

In the mean time with her good luck she received a letter from her cousin at Modinagar who wrote," the driver of the motor Riksha wrote and communicated through a newspaper that someone forgot some documents in his scooter (Motor Riksha) back seat". Her cousin brother also wrote her that he had already contacted the Riksha driver and claimed that those documents belong to her sister. He agreed to get those documents and pay some reward for that.

Ryan, your Nanni went ahead and paid whatever this scooter (Motor Riksha0 driver wanted her to pay. This scooter driver was not highly educated. He showed the documents to someone else who could understand those documents. This guy told him that these documents had no value or benefit to him and the best thing for him to find the person whom they belong and hand over to them. It could be possible that the person might give you some reward or monetary compensation for your efforts and honesty. This motivated him (The driver) to give in the newspaper and try to find the real owner of those documents. Baljit's cousin brother happened to read the news in Modinagar and communicated to your Nanni. Your Nanni left Panjab immediately to reach Modinagar and she was prepared to fulfill the conditions of this scooter driver. Modinagar was in UP or Uttar Pradesh state of India and it took her about seven –eight hours in buses and trains. After she reached in the area around New Delhi and in Uttar Pradesh where that driver lived, she approached the guy and gave him a few hundred rupees as his reward for doing what he did and he gave her the visa documents. She was very happy to resolve the problem and started making arrangements to come to USA and join me. She acted very strongly and stayed positive and did not abandon her efforts. She finally became hopeful by God's grace. Finally she decided to say farewell to my parents. My father decided to see them off at the railway station. He was very attached to your Aunti Dipika as she was very small and only a few months old when she came to stay with him. He took care of her when your Nanni was busy in doing house hold work. She would always want to go back to my dad and he would pick her and take her out. They were both very happy with each other. Dipika always would crawl on floor to get him as she was not walking yet and he would pick her and take her out. Finally the day came when your Nanni, Your aunti Dipika and your mom had to leave to come to USA and my dad came to railway station of Patiala to see them off with his best wishes. I simply learnt from your Nanni that it was a very emotional scene at the railway station. My dad was standing outside on the railway platform close to the train window and Dipika had her arms open to go to him. My dad was crying and so was your auntie Dipika. The scene was very sensational and the train was whistling to start and there were some tears on the platform as well as in side the train compartment. Dipika had her arms open and wanted to go to my dad and her arms were out through the railway train window to go to my dad. Some lady who was witnessing all this asked your Nanni who was that man outside on the platform? Was he your dad? She said," No, he is my father in law". The lady remarked," Never saw such an attachment between a baby and a grand papa. He must be a wonderful person and must have loved his granddaughters a lot as he is standing out there and crying for them as well as for you". My father was in tears when they were all leaving for USA. Perhaps that is the way we all get attached to our children and grandchildren and anyone else we get attached to either through our family relationship and even our friendship relations.

I had already sent tickets through TWA for her and she scheduled her as well as Komal and Dipika's flight to come to USA. Unfortunately a war broke out between India and Pakistan and all airports were kept dark as a defense measure. Your Nanni, your mom and your auntie Dipika left Mumbai airport in a declared war when India and Pakistan were in a War" Dark Out" when all the lights were off and the airport looked like a ghost town. This was in late seventies when war was in progress between India and Pakistan. She did not see Mumbai and she simply heard about it. Some time I feel the warring nations should have a proper way and rules to fight among nations and fighting practices should pay attention to save human life of children, women and old peoples of any country and of any religion, color or culture or the nationalities. Any terrorism and extremist activities to destroy the basic humanity must be dealt with very seriously and strongly by not only by USA government but by all the governments and rulers around the world in case the human race has to survive on this planet so called Earth. I feel that it is always the small number who always try to damage and destroy a peace loving society and humanity almost all over the world irrespective of any cultural, religious beliefs or philosophy of ruling the masses.

She (my wife) made to USA and reached Boston airport along with my two little angels, your mom and your auntie Dipika. She was looking forward to see me and your mom and auntie were as well also excited to see their dad. She had no idea how far she was still from Ohio. She knew she had to take another flight for another two to two and a half hour.

At Boston your nannie missed her flight to Cincinnati just by a few minutes. She had to stay in a hotel along with your mom and auntie. On the other side I was very excited to see and receive all of them. I went to Cincinnati airport with my friend Jack and his wife Audie to receive and pick them (Your mom, your auntie Dipika and your Nannie). But they could not make it. She called me from the airport that she missed her flight

Your Nannie stayed in a Hotel as directed by the airline. She called me from there and I had no idea how she did and she told me that she would be there tomorrow instead of today. I kidded her saying," Just remember I paid for your airfare and wanted my daughters here with me". She laughed and was going through her own communication problems with hotel peoples She was very much worried about your mom and your auntie such as what to feed them. She could not communicate for what to eat herself and what she could order for her daughters and had no idea what she could ask for both of them. Your mom was only two and half year old and your auntie Dipika was only ten months old. I said, OK, do not worry you will come tomorrow and I have been informed by TWA ".

She was going through some communication difficulties at the hotel she was staying in. At least that was what everyone around her was thinking. It was partially my fault. As I told the airline that she might not be able to speak in English. The airline people were communicating with her in sign language. Here on the other end Baljit was thinking why I was being treated as a total UN educated in English. It was all my fault as I told them that she did not know any English. Actually it was my own fears that my family might get lost on way. I was simply wanted them to take care.

Next morning, your Nannie took shuttle from the hotel to airport. The shuttle dropped her at the east Boston airport. Her flight was departing from West airport. Your nannie was very confused with two little babies with her. Airline hostesses smiled at her while she was trying to figure out what to do. It was a positive influence on her and uplifted her. Her flight was departing from western airport. She was very stressed out with two little ones with her to figure out what TO DO. A LADY FROM NO WHERE asked her to come with her as she was going to westerner airport herself. Sometime I feel USA people are not only wonderful but they are the one God chose to help the suffering humans all around the globe to help the sufferers from all kind of evils existing in this world. I know people do not believe in God but sometimes he appears in a very unique and special way as a human like us. She took ride from her and reached the right side of the airport and could get the flight to Cincinnati airport via Petersburg. PA.

TWA airline was very courteous and allowed me to go to airplane and receive your Nannie, your mom and your auntie Dipika. THANK GOD we were together again. Your Nannie was holding your mom and your auntie was …I asked your Nannie where was Dipika? She was totally changed as I left her. She was dressed in Green and looked so white to me and was in the arms of air hostess. I could not believe how she looked as a wonderful happy baby. My breath almost stopped looking on my family especially your nannie, your mom and your auntie Dipika.

I lived in a small apartment in Middletown Ohio. Our apartment was upstairs in a two story apartment complex in down town Middletown. It was the month of December and the tenth day of 1971 and was getting cold and when our family got united again. Your mom and your auntie were very energetic to know what was going on. It snowed and there was snowflakes all over the area we were looking. Your mom and your auntie were very curious and wanted to see snow which they never saw before. Next morning it was still snowing. I went to my work early in the morning and so did my close friend who was living with me before they came. Your nannie, your mom and auntie Dipika were in the apartment just by themselves. Your mom and auntie Dipika, they both sneaked out of the apartment while your Nannie was doing some house chores in the Kitchen probably cooking, her best hobby, she always stayed on top of it. No one in our family had ever gone hungry since she came to our home or more correctly in her home. They both stepped into the snow and were totally barefooted and were feeling the falling snow outside. Dipika was so curious to know more about where they were that she kept walking further in snow on the second floor which was open from one side and she was younger but could walk of her own in a couple of inches of snow drifted on the second floor. She stepped over the stairway which was open and she started falling from the stair and clang herself holding the step which were of painted metal. Your mom came running to the apartment and told your nannie that Dipika was falling from stairway steps. Your Nannie came running and rescued her. In the evening she told me that we should shift to ground floor apartment for our girl's safety. I talked to my landlord who managed to shift us to a ground floor apartment with in a few days.

Sam, I just found out that you would be getting a plastic cast on your both arms. You did not even do anything such as a fall or any sport injury extra. Poor you! Doctors wanted you to keep your arms straight and that, s all. You had been brave with doctors, nurses and hospitals before. You know that they always tried to do their best to comfort you. I am very sure you would go through this without any major problem. You have always fought to survive.

Let us go back to our other story which you were listening to so attentively. Finally we got an apartment on the ground floor. These were Malburry's apartments in Midddletown Ohio. In this apartment we had even a back yard where your mom and your auntie could play. In about a year later your uncle Surej was born while we were living in that apartment. This was only two bed room apartment. Your mom and your auntie Dipika were very happy to have their little brother. They loved to take care him and feed him and we had no one or knew anyone else to take care him. We were going through tough time going around as a family as we were five of us. I decided to buy a brand new car 'Nova' to facilitate going around with the family as I had no knowledge of cars used or new ones. It was spring of 1975 and it rained so much that whole town of Middletown was flooded. Our apartment was next to a creek which got over flooded and so was our apartment and the parking lot as we were on the ground floor. There was about two to three feet of water in the parking lot and the water was coming through in our apartment.

I took your mom and your auntie to a neighbor, an old lady Francis who loved them and saw them playing in the back yard. She was very nice and she asked me to bring them upstairs. As soon as I came down after leaving them with her, I noticed my new car was floating and drifting in water in parking lot. I was feeling devastated. Fortunately fire brigade people noticed me struggling to contain my car and the car was almost ready to float away. I was totally perplexed and had no idea what to do. The fire men helped me in tying my car to a steel column of the apartment building to secure from float away in high water. It was very scary. These two firemen were of them which I could never know their names or addresses to send them a THANK YOU note. I know now that most of them are simply volunteers and deserve Praise AND Gratitude in our day to day life. All of us feel secured and safe with their existence and work they do. Your Nannie was alone in the apartment and was trying to save our belongings as the water was coming and rising in our apartment. As soon as I opened the front door, the whole flood water started coming into our living room and our whole furniture was under water. Luckily the water did not reach our bedrooms. Our beds were still dry and OK. At that time I had no idea about any kind of flood insurance either. After a few hours the flood water started going down. I brought your mom and auntie Dipika down to our own apartment. We all ate some left over food and went to sleep in our beds. Your Nannie kept your uncle Surej with her all this time as I took your mom and Auntie on second floor to Francis.

When we were living in that apartment, one day your Nannie got tired she fell sleep in the day. Your mom and your auntie were playing and tried to fix some lunch for themselves to eat in the kitchen. Both of them were very adventurous and daring and of taking charge of any situation. That was just my guess. Actually I had no idea what they were doing. It was a little after midday. Some way they turned the electric range on to warm something. A paper towel was lying close to the range which caught fire suddenly. Your mom picked that and through in the trash bin. The trash bin caught fire and smoke was all over in the kitchen. At that point your mom woke your Nannie up saying," Mommy, Mommy-Fire, and Fire". Your Nannie got up and took care of the fire by throwing some water in the trash can and opened the back door to get rid of the smoke.

Sam, your Nannie was always very swift in case of a mishap and a problem. I was always very slow and felt inadequate without her presence. I always felt insufficient and sometime even inferior against her practicality in such situations. I always felt that someday she would leave me because she would think I am too dumb for her. She had always been too smart and practical in day to day living. In our household I never did much and she took care of about everything. I was very easy going and laid back and let her take the stressful jobs in home like paying bills and invoices. I always wanted to take at ease as any stress would create an Asthma attack. So I always managed to stay away from stressful personal situations. Your Nanni always took over such tasks, I was not able to fight with anyone but she would give the person in same coin to their face. I always felt secure in the background.

Sam, I got to tell you a little funny story for you to laugh at. As you know I was working on a small contract and I was staying in a motel as I was about two hours' drive from home. This motel was about twenty miles from my work place. Your nannie suggested that go closer to your work place and rent another motel closer to my work place. I finally found one and in the same town of Cambridge I was working in. This was owned by one of the Indian and he was a Patel from Gujrat India. He took about two weeks to give the room in his motel. I stopped at his motel couple of time to find if he had a vacancy. Second time he said," Yes, I do and come tomorrow and get the key". Next day again on my way from work I stopped in the evening and he gave the key of the room to look over and also told me that due to a storm in town there was no electric in the motel but should come any time that evening".

I took the key and proceeded to see the room as per his directions. It was evening around seven pm, I opened the room but could not see much due to darkness and without any light due to a power outage. The location of the motel was very suitable to me as it was only two /three miles from work place and I could see furniture in the room as well as sheets on the bed and towels in the room. I just trusted my old countryman, Patel. I did tell his wife that my nephew (Deepak) was married to a Patel girl named Gargi and some way I was related to them. I told her that I would move in next day from other motel. Next day, during my lunch time I moved in and gave him in advance for the whole month. He was very happy to have me there.

In the evening, after work I came to my room. To my surprise, I found all the furniture in a very poor condition. Table had no drawers. There was a place for hanging my clothes but it was in front of the refrigerator doors I hanged my clothes but every time I would open the refrigerator, I had to touch all the ironed clothes with the door of the refrigerator. The refrigerator was just a small one and was placed on the top of an old table. The microwave was very old but was working. There was a table which was very shaky and chairs were shaky and old sofa was also cramped into the room. The room was hardly 8ft by 12ft and lot of extra furniture was stacked in the room. There was a shelf made in the room about 2-1/2 ft. on one wall next to the refrigerator which was just hand made with very old wood.

The bathroom was cramped and had a standing shower and on the bathroom walls there was green scales which made me clear that it had not seen a cleaning person for that room. Next day I also found out that was a smoking room and the previous occupant had left some holes of burns on sofa as well as bed cover had marks and holes of smoke damage. I also found some roaches in the bathroom running around and on the walls close to my bed. Ryan, it was scary for me to sleep and was just wondering that there might be some bed bugs too. These motel owners had no concern and was wondering how the health department let such motels to stay open. Next morning I complained to the owner about my concerns and he promised that he would change my room as soon as someone vacates. There was lot of oil and gas fracking and drilling business going on this area and lot of contractors and workers were living in motels and hotels on a temporary basis like me. The owner promised he would keep me in mind that if any better, non-smoking room vacancy occurred, he would give me and move me to that room. I was worried about my food in the refrigerator which I used to bring for the whole week from your nannie that I might be sharing with those roaches as I found one in my small refrigerator. Next evening again after work I stopped at motel office and talked to Mr. Patel. He said," All my rooms have been damaged by customers who smoked. Even my non-smoking rooms are damaged by smoke". I found out these owners do not care and they only need their rent. I had already paid him for the whole month and he had already a sign in office and in Lobby "No Refunds". I felt taken in by my own countryman from Gujrat, India but felt happy to be alive and witness these things. Every morning, I woke up with roaches running around to wish me Good Morning and they were all around me and I did not even kill any roaches who were sharing my room with me in the motel and were my room mates for a few weeks. This founded secret I kept with me and never told anyone except you Ryan! The funniest thing I found that these roaches and bugs cannot be killed even by micro wave. One day I wanted to warm my food in Microwave oven and found a roach sitting inside and would not come out. I thought I should kill it by microwaving. So I turned the microwave oven on for two minutes. It was still running around. It was possible that it needed bigger doze of microwave. One day I found one in my refrigerator. These creatures can live in all temperatures such as cold or heat. Nothing seems to bother them. Finally I had to kill the one in my refrigerator and I had no idea how long he was sharing my food which your nannie made only for me. She always thought that she was only making food for me and she had no idea of my numerous roommates.

SAM laughed with me. He knew what I was talking about. Couple of days later my room was cleaned. I opened my room when I came from work, there was my bed totally made and sheets were changed. I was very happy to see the change until I found my shaving kit case had been moved from bathroom to my room. The shaving kit case was opened but nothing stolen or taken away. There were some apples which I had in a bag and they were found opened. I was wondering that they were in a bag and were opened. Nothing was lost or stolen but something had changed which I could not understand what? I noticed that roaches were running all over in bathroom and on cabinets, on refrigerators and all around on tables around my bed. I started killing them and as I would go to bathroom roaches would come under my feet and get killed. Sometimes I would think that this form of life had been created by nature or God and I should not kill them. But I did kill them when they invaded my territory. I started thinking moving to some other motel, but I had already paid next month rent and the owner my motel owner, Indian country man had a sign", No refunds". Actually I was not worried about the refunds. I just wanted to survive under the circumstances as probably exactly what they (Roaches) were trying to do. The motel owner had been keeping my room air conditioner on all the time and was set on about 63 degrees Fahrenheit. In cold all roaches were either getting killed or they were just hiding in those wood paneled walls. It had been about a month and I was getting used to these roaches and bugs. Some time I would get mad at these roaches when they would invade my territory. I killed a few of them and broke laws of nonviolence set by Buddha, other prophets, and Gandhi. I went out couple of evenings looking for another motel what in that town there was no vacancy and they put me on waiting list.

Some morning when I put my cup of tea in the microwave oven to prepare for microwaved tea, I would see a roach in the microwave oven. I turned it on to kill but nothing would happen to this tiny creature. May they do not get killed right away but sometime later? Finally at the end of the month the motel owner changed my room to a bigger room. There were no roaches in that room but a small window air conditioner. So I took a fan from home to stay cool. A week later your nannie fell from stairs in the basement and I turned in a request and I had to quit my job on account of family situation. This was around 2015 of February,

Samuel, I am sorry I have not told you about your story. I know your and mine story are not different. Your story is not complete without mine story and same way my story is totally in complete without your story. We are both integral part of each other. Ryan, laughed loudly. I wished if he could speak to me in normal language but his smiles and zesters told me about his thinking. Sam, from now on I would only tell you about your own story and the things pertain to you. Sam just laughed and communicated to me his happiness to listen my story. May be my story was boring and your story would be more interesting for you.

This was around beginning of 1975 and I decided to change my job to private sector from government job and I got a better job offer from a rural electric company from Butler, Ohio which was even we bought a house in Middletown and we did not even move into that house. We all along with your mom, auntie Dipika and uncle Surej moved to rural area of Fitch Ville, Ohio which is north of Ohio, south west of Cleveland.

We all were very happy as people were wonderful and help us to adjust in that area. People were very courteous. My children found friends very easily and their friend's family trusted us with their children staying at our home. My children had no friend from India contrary to what happens in big cities but they were all happy and well adjusted. I was feeling great as USA is a country where caste and class and some one's religion had no significance for establishing relationships or other barriers. My children and we ourselves did not feel isolated from other peoples. We lived in wonderful peoples of rural background and they all helped us to raise our children in a better and a safe way as we were.

Sam, I am only telling you this story because I want you to know how and what happened when you were born. Your mom, your auntie Dipika and your uncle Surej were all with your mom and dad. Let me tell you how it all happened for your mom and dad and most importantly about you.

Sam, your mom, your auntie Dipika and your uncle graduated from Fitch Ville High School. Your auntie Dipika went to university of Michigan and your mom and your uncle Surej went to University of Ohio. Your mom found your dad Bill in Ohio State University and we saw your dad Bill in our house in Fitch Ville. We saw him and later his parents in Columbus, Ohio at a restaurant. They were all seemed as wonderful people and I believe they are. We agreed about their marriage together and they both got married in Columbus, Ohio. We were all happy about their relationship. We met your dad's side family. They were all wonderful people and I believe them as wonderful peoples as I met them all and sometimes I still see them on my grandchildren games. Your grandpa Hennery and your grandma Linda were really good people. Your aunties Susie and her elder sisters and their family were all great.

Sam, you were born after their marriage. On August 21, 1997 and you brought joy to all our family and friends, we never asked more from God. You were the answer to our prayers for our family. You were very cute and a smiling baby. Our whole family loved and welcomed you in the family, especially your nanny and I as you were our first grandson. You are our special grandson and we never feel you to be of your own special needs. Although we had to admit that you are our special need grandchild and happened to be our first grands child. We love you the way you are and thank God for his miracle upon us and upon our family.

We all had fun with you all the time. Your mom and dad were both working and needed a baby sitter for you for days only. They stayed with you until you were about three months old approximately. They both loved you very much and were not enthusiastic to leave with a baby sitter. After checking a few baby sitters in Columbus area, they found one to leave you with who took care of other babies too. Your mom and your dad wanted to try that babysitter for a day to see how you would like. Your mom was just planning to go back to her job after her maternity leave in case she could find the babysitter where you feel comfortable with. Your dad was already back to his work at Ohio State. Your nannie and I was in Springfield, Ohio and also were both working.

This was around mid-November of 1997 and you were only about a weak short of completing your first three months of your life. Your nanny woke me up almost sleeping at mid night and she said," Get up and listen," Komal is crying and conveyed the message on phone that Sam is in the hospital. He was carried there in an ambulance and is in ICU". Your nanny was ready to leave right away but it was dark and almost mid night AND SHE GOT A CALL FROM YOUR

Grandma Linda called your nanny not to go in during night and go early in the morning. She agreed but I had no idea whether she went to sleep after that or not. She left first thing in the morning to be with you and told her that I would be with you next day as I was working next morning. She kept me informed your condition to me almost every hour and she was with you.

Next day I got up and woke up and went to temple and told about your episode to the priest of our Hindu Temple AND HE gave me the holly water to give you and he prayed with me for your survival.

I was there in the hospital to see you along with my Bhagwat Gita. I saw you hooked with all kind of cables and wirings which were all aimed at keeping you serving to live. Next morning as I reached to see you in the hospital, I found you hooked up to different equipment's. I sat right next you to pray and read my Bhagwat Gita and remember just opening the book simply with prayer to make you OK.

I was very much impressed by your baby sitter and his family as they were concerned about your survival too. She and her family was also sitting in the Sam's hospital room and they were all very much worried about your survival. That was the time I found out that you were in your babysitter's basement along with other babies she was taking care that day. That was the first day and the last day you ever spent with a baby sitter.

Due to some God's grace you were selected to survive but differently and in a special need baby. You stopped breathing and went into deep sleep and no one could figure out how long you did not breathe but with the great work of ambulance workers who kept you alive and you were taken to Columbus Children Hospital where you recovered for about a week before the doctor released you to come to home. But in this episode you lost your motor skills which were per mentally and permanently damaged in your cardiac arrest stage. The doctors only said you were the victim of SID (Sudden Infant Death Syndrome), which I never heard about that before this happening. It was a cardiac arrest in your deep sleep as you only sounded like simply sleeping to your baby sister and you stopped breathing and had some damage to your brain. You lost your motor skills along with skills to eat yourself and for your own survival. Doctors and hospitals made you a tube fed baby as you were not able to eat yourself. Since than you have always been fed through a tube already planted in your stomach.

Sam, we were thankful to god who at least kept you alive under these episodes. You still retained your smile. Although you could not move your legs and arms as you wished but you could smile for everyone who so ever wanted to talk to you. I remember when I took you to some public places such as shopping malls, the women would stop and see your wide eyes and tell me," what an adorable child". I could not feel happier. Sam, you made many lives happier by making everyone around you happy and loving.

Sam, today you are already eighteen year old and had a social function in your high school. Your Mommy and your Nanny were with you in school. Your Nanny was kind enough to cut some vegetables such as onions, green pepper and tomatoes for me for my dinner. She told me to get pizza out of the frizz and put these vegetables on the pizza AND PUT IT IN THE OVEN. I SAID OK, OK I SHALL I would make it. You can go and enjoy with Sam AND MY Daughter Komal your mom. At about 7:00Pm I brought a pepperoni pizza from the frizz and opened the box and spread all the cut vegetables on it. Your nannie was complaining also to keep the house clean and not to make mess. I opened the pizza box and placed frozen Pizza on a pizza baking tray and spread all vegetables SHE CUT on the pizza. I threw the pizza box and card board in Recyclable bin. I turned on the oven on bake at 400 degree F. I placed the pizza on the rack. I had no idea what further to be done. I already threw the box and went after the recyclable bin to find the box and read the directions. I could not find that box in that big recyclables things. Now my pizza is in the oven and I don't know when I should take it out. I kept on looking into the oven every minute. I did not see anything unusual, but I am also looking for the box to find the time to cook and other directions.

Sam, don't laugh at me. I was simply trying to make my pizza. I knew that Ryan always like my stories. Finally when I saw my pizza almost burnt. I took it out of the oven. It was over crunchy and slightly black but I ate it before your nannie came and with my own surprise I found that I even did not remove the card board under the pizza and pizza crust was all baked with the card board under the pizza and I had to peel off the card board which was itself a job," but when you are hungry, you would do anything to survive and will eat anything." I was afraid what she would say and tried to hide my pizza but as soon as she came and saw that pizza.

Sam, you are not only my first grandson but my inspiration in my life. You can laugh with me even if nothing is there to laugh about. You give me the sense of real life. Whenever I get really fed up and frustrated from life I usually come and see you without calling your mom or dad. You are my only inspiration to live on and keep on connecting the world around me. My inner world in my own self as well as my outer world is connected through you. Your happiness and smiles is my treasure I cherish. Some time I wonder how many more children have gone through this kind of life changing event. I wish them well and my heart goes for each and every one along with their family suffering from this kind of problem my suggestion to all of them is that God has chosen you for reason to be parent or related to a child like this. Simply enjoy them and cherish them as God given gift. I know that these kind of children are born to teach us the value of life and teach us about the real love. The other day in my own neighborhood I saw a girl on an walker like you used to have and she was trying to walk and I saw her and could not help clapping and backing her up saying," Great job, great job and you are doing great." She got excited and started walking faster and faster. I did not know exactly the lady accompanied her whether she was her mom or a sitter but she told me that no one had ever encouraged and cheered her like this and that what motivated her to walk with her walker. I told her that I also have a grandson in this kind of situation and I love them as my own.

Today your mom married your step dad Joe who also love you very much and you were smiling all along the ceremony. Tony also read some verses before they took their vowels to each other. Sam, you were composed and collected and did not show any emotions. You and all of us met Joe's family and all of them were very happy to meet you Sam, you smiled with each and every one present there that day.

Sam, you and Tony are very strong boys who have faced a set back of a broken family and you having your health and special need issues, both of you brothers(Sam and Tony) survived very successfully and faced everything strongly and with reality. We are very much proud of you both. Sam and Tony are both exceptional brothers. Tony loves his older brother Sam very much. I have noticed many times their love for each other which is probably due to my daughter and your mom Komal and how she raised both and you Sam! Both of you should be proud of your mom who loved you both dearly in spite of her own life problems. Both of you can stay in touch with your dad too. I am sure he also love you both in his own way. He loves you both. The whole world love TONY and SAM even if the whole world does not know you but everyone knows that can happen with children and that is why God has given them the greatest resilience and much more than adults. No one knows that you guys even started a Brother's Day and showed a great love for each other. I wish every family should have and celebrate a brother's day and it may and can differ family to family and should have a goal to advance more and more love among brothers and sisters.

Sam/Tony and all my other grand children from my brother side of the family (Jack, Nate, Ezabel, Lilya, Dhilan and Blake) I simply wanted both of you to know that your Nanna did not come to USA for making more money but actually the real free life and the best of everything you can imagine and its ideology towards human being all over planet. It always surprised me if someone showed me a dissatisfaction living in this country. I always felt telling them you need to go to some another country and you might just change your mind. When I was working for electrical utilities,sometime some of our customers will complain a short discomfort of not having electric for a very short time and some of them would say to me that you are from India and that is why you don't know how fast electric should come in this country. But that always made me more efficient and made me more understandable about their needs. Those utility customers always made me more aggressive and sympathetic about the life which get effected so fast with things which we have become accustomed to. sAM, next couple of pages I shall not talk to you until you are at least twenty one year old and same goes for Griffin. Both of you should not read these pages unless you guys are over twenty one year old.

This was about early nineteen eighties and this was my second job in Ohio at New London. The first one was at Lebanon Ohio. I moved to New London with the help of my friend Jack. This was after I had already worked on that job for about six years. Your Nanni decided to go back to work. Until that time she was busy in raising children that is your mom, auntie Dipika and Uncle Surej. She took some adult education courses in Nursing. After about three months of classes she got certified as a Nursing Assistant and she got the job in hospital in Norwalk Ohio. She got the job in third shift because she wanted to take care of her day duties such as picking children from school and dropping me and picking me from work as we had only one car for all of us five. Your Nanni was gone at nights to her work AND I WAS STAYING WITH your mom, auntie and uncle Surej. Life was going on great but stressful.

Right in those days my father and your great Grand Father died suddenly with a heart attack and it all happened in India and I could not even be there for his last moments to take care of him and do anything for his last time. After about two weeks his cremation ceremony I got a letter about his death which was almost as per Indian customs to inform kith and kinks after certain number of days of death. I was not only devastated but totally paralyzed with news I got from my eldest brother. I was simply crying at my heart for a few days and could not go to work. My work place people sent me flowers and I was crying like a child. That day I found out that I never grew up like a man. I missed my dad bad and decided to go and see my mom. I was in a grieving stage.

Just prior to all this, there was a Christmas Party of my company where I met the wife of my contractor. She and her husband sat right next to me and your nannie. She asked if I can take her to an upcoming school of custom chemical applicators in Cleveland. I said," Just call me next week and I shall let you know if I can". Next day my manager asked me to go to that school as I was holding license for the company to use pesticides for vegetation controls under electric lines. I registered myself in that state sponsored seminar in Cleveland. Week later I got a call from tree contractor's wife …Susie………. Who asked me for taking her to the custom applicator's school? I agreed. She said," I shall come in the evening at your house and shall follow you to Cleveland". She did come to my house a night before our training seminar. She stayed in the driveway in her car. She came and knocked our door and went back to her car. I got out and talked to her and said let me pick my briefcase and small suitcase and I would be out and drive to Cleveland. She kept her car running. Baljit was very busy in cooking for children and I told her I would grab something to eat on my way and told her that someone was waiting for me in the driveway. She was also under a great pressure to go to her job as well as taking care of children. KOMAL is a very strong girl and DIPIKA and SUREJ was also getting stronger and stronger and we never felt inadequate leaving them alone in a small town where everybody new everybody else. This is a town where I felt most comfortable and secure living in. The people in this town were so nice and great who never left us feeling that we were not in our own home town. People were very simple, honest and did not discriminate us as from other part of the world. My children could find easily friends and they could visit their house and they were all welcomed in our house. That is the time I actually started believing in the phrase that "it takes a village to raise a child" as village of Fitchville, Ohio did raise my children into good responsible citizens of US.

She (My Electrical contractor's wife, Susie kept her car running as it was cold weather and I came out with my brief case and a small suitcase. She said," Please follow me or she would follow my truck" I sat in my truck and started following her. After a few hundred yard she pulled out and told me that it would be easier for her not to drive separately. She asked if she could park her car and just ride with me. I said," OK, you can park your car at my company parking lot and I shall pick you from there". She did exactly the same and I picked her from company parking lot and from there on we were in the same vehicle which was my company truck and I was allowed to use as on being used on company business and I was using that almost every day on my work.

Tonight was different and we were both travelling in my truck. She indicated that she had no reservation in any hotel. I said ok I would check with the Marriot where I would be staying and there might be vacancy there. We reached Cleveland at Marriot Hotel and found they had a vacancy and she signed for that and we both checked in for the night. After that we both went to our rooms. After about fifteen minutes after we both checked in, she called me in my room that I get to get something to eat and she said I am hungry. I said," OK, I shall see you in hotel lobby and we shall go out to get something to eat."

At around 9:00 PM we both went out to a restaurant which was about couple of miles from our hotel. We both ordered food and drinks. While sitting just across of each other we were both looking into each other eyes and were very happy. We finished our food and checked out. We went back to our hotel. She asked if I would like to go for a walk in parking lot of the hotel. I said, "OK that will be fine". We both were walking in the parking lot and it was a moonlight light. She hugged me and I kissed her. We were both involved at that time and as we came back to hour hotel lobby she invited me to her room. That was the start of our affair. She expressed that she wanted to see me at least once a week which I did for about two or three months when I was at fieldwork of my job.

This was my own weakness and nobody else. I was the one board and did not know how to get over it. Finally your nannie found out through catching up one of my letter from her. I was in bad situation. My relationship with my own family, my children was totally devastated to an irreparable damage. Even today there was nothing except sufferings and misunderstandings in my own family. Only thing I even know today for sure is that I love each and every one of them. They all have given me nothing but happiness. I did give them hurt and I could not go back and undo anything of my inappropriate behavior. I am not a role model and just an ordinary human being governed by human nature. Only thing I can say about my family is that I love them and I will not be able do without any one of them. They are all my blood and soul. Also I only want peace and love for the woman and her family I was involved with. She was wonderful and never tried to damage my family. I kept on giving contracts to her husband which she wanted indirectly. Later on her husband died with a heart attack and I did not do anything to abandon her company or cut down any ones work load as compared to other contractors. I did whatever my general manager wanted me to do. Finally we both decided and promised not to hurt each other family and continue our lives in peace and harmony. We decided to detach and break up at no terms in the interest of our respective family members. We both stopped all communications with each other.

However as my general manager wanted me to penalize for having an affair with a contractor's wife and I was suspended from job for four days. I suffered and suffered those four days and had no one to blame for. It was all my fault and I took full responsibility of what happened in that part of my life. My company got me back to job after four days of my suspension.

Baljit was very upset. She beat me with a bat and shoes and I could not see her hurt in her heart but only could feel in my own heart. I cherished her beatings as she was my most loving relationship I ever had in my whole life. Touching her was just touching my own body and feeling comfortable in my own body. But she had been effected by recent events and I could not blame her for anything. Even today after about twenty years later she shows her hurt and sometimes pick her shoe to hit me and I get angry too. I know I cannot kill her too for my own mistake and she could not forgive me and continue with her grudge which pops up many times in a day. There is nothing I can do to unwind the clock and simply repent on my own actions and ask for forgiveness of what I did to her. I know due to my own mistake, she is not the same person which I married. She is great and I still love her. She is not dependent on me but I am the one dependent on her. SAM, your Nanni is a very independent woman. She loves eating from her own two hands which simply means she believes in working for everything she decides to eat. Sam simply smiled. She is a hard worker and a consequently I sought myself to drinking to continue my survival in despair. Now I am nothing but an addict and depressed from my own life as I lost everything I lived for in my life. Even psychological counseling went in wane. But down there in my deep heart I still love her and do not want to lose her under any condition even I know she is very bitter. Her communications with me are nothing but harsh and degrading. Although I always try to keep myself and my mind busy in doing things but I still do not know how I can keep myself happy and contained and finish the feeling of loneliness and emptiness within me. Only time I feel happy is when I see my Ryan and he laughs with me on little and small jokes. I always love to have counting from one to one hundred with him and that make us both happy. Our relationship is definitely not of a grand pa and a grandson but friends who love each other without any requirement or stiff rules built by society or any government but a relationship based upon plain love or likings. SAM is now 18 years old and I ask him regularly on almost every other day that Nanna wants to know everything what you did in school and I want to know even about your friends. Were they boys are girls and Ryan just smiles all the time. I usually tell him that no keeping secrets from Nanna, he laughs loudly and get excited to say or speak something. That is our best moment I always love it.

If we definitely believe in Love why we do hate? Does God if we believe in him tell us to hate or love? The fact is hate will not take you anywhere and your hurts would continue in your own self and will multiply and multiply. So give up and surrender yourself to GOD and enjoy your life which God has given you and always believe he did not create you to punish you but reward you for what you did well and forgive your shortcoming. Some might call this as a KARMA or whatever you do or perform would be given back to you as a reaction of nature. Which seems great, if you do well you will be rewarded with good and if do bad you will be rewarded in return whatever you deserve.

Sam, to me life is just a journey in a train probably in India or in USA. You can only select where to stop and get down or board without having any control over START and ENDING of your train journey which has already been programmed. We should always be grateful to Almighty who provided this train ride which goes around and around. All our STOPS, BOARD or UNBOARD are simply our own KARMAS or actions which can be positive or negatives and consequently can become exciting or depressive. SAM, I always become highly curious to know what makes you smile and happy always.

Although we humans are not supposed to judge anyone and who we think judges all the time to almost eight billion people on this planet. Certainly all mighty God has other important things to do such as making sure all the planets, sun and moon and other objects do stick to His schedule and the rules of his nature. Probably that is why an apple has never gone up in sky but to earth only when it get matured. I believe that he left humans to judge for themselves to make right decisions before doing actions or doing any karma. God may or may not react to what you are doing to other peoples around you. Your own Karma or deeds will come and serve you positively or negatively.

SAM, when I look back people told me that America is a MELTING POT where all nationalities and people of all religions and beliefs join and get cooked together and blend with each other without barriers and form and color of their skin, their origin. That is why I love this country of United States of America and I call my home and my children and grand children's home and feel comfortable in living here and fight for the people who live here and I know many friends who feel the same way too and some responsibilities go along with a citizenship. This is the only country which let you carry your own belief system and traditions which was confirmed by the Toledo court judge who gave my wife the citizenship rights. Dal was selected to give a speech in his court, "Why do you choose to become an USA citizen?"

I know that immigration is a big issue in our country especially in this coming election but it is all about sharing the planet of earth to live in harmony among us as well as all other living things on this earth which include all insects, all animals and vegetation life on this earth we call it a GLOBE. God did not make boarders mankind did. I am really grateful for our country United States of America, and its generosity and its real sense of properties and qualities of a so called "MELTING POT" country values. I wish the whole world and its countries should have believed in the ideology of AMERICAN peoples and stay away from wars for their selfish reasons and damaging the poor and destitute in their missions to resettle wherever they want to. I, my children and grandchildren are all proud to be Americans and I am really grateful for our immigration policy and I would prefer everyone to come in legally and follow the rules of law. When I see my own family along with my brother's family, I can see and really feel that our family is definitely a Melting Pot family I understand the controversy of and should be decided by vetting process of the country amination of any designated or selected political party of the company and the general human survival needs and keeping in mind that USA is the only lead in the world for the poor and the human right problems in the world. As some of the countries are ruled by dictators and simply selfish rulers hungry for their own power who ignore the view and needs of common peoples. I am grateful for the good will of the USA constitution along with its peoples who have very great immigration and naturalization Laws for the peoples of the world from all over the world.

Although I do believe that state of the world situation has changed a lot due to prevalent terrorism activities increasing all over the world and USA should increase the scrutinizing and vetting process but that should not make us believe that everyone coming to USA is a terrorist and continue its policies for refugees especially for neutral children and women who simply need help to survive under some situations caused by unrest and wars in certain countries. It is not possible that every refugee would turn out to be a Terrorist in future or currently a terrorist. Although it is possible to deceive and cheat US system of immigration for such activities. That is where our challenge lies to administrate and execute laws of immigration with great carefulness. On the whole USA has a very generous immigration rules for right people to come and work in the country on a very fair conditions. There is nothing wrong in tightening these laws and some more vetting and checking more the immigrants coming in this country. USA should be careful and more vigilant about anyone trying to manipulate its laws to damage the people of USA. These type of people should be kept out of the country at all cost. This may and may not be correct that ninety percent of the legal immigrants coming to USA are not terrorist or coming to damage the country people and are simply human beings suffering from dictators ruling their country and ignoring all human rights for ordinary peoples of their own countrymen or too selfish and ignore all needs of the peoples. However I am for strict rules of immigration and a thorough check up before issuing a visa for the country even if it is just a visitor visa. These are just normal checkup procedures based upon human safety and as well as on the protection of US citizens. I do feel that to achieve this is not an ordinary effort but will take extra ordinary efforts to make this happen in today's world where people can easily fool others. Sometimes bad or terrorist people try to sabotage the system which makes genuine immigrants more difficulties and hardships. Some may be genuine refugees and some may be wanted professionals such as Nurses, doctors and engineers.

Sam! You have taught me a lot about humanity and the life. You have taught me the real value of a smile without asking nothing and selfless caring for others and humanity. Human race does not comprise only the healthy, rich and powerful but also of sick, poor and week. We should not go by the rule of the jungle where powerful only survives and some accepts this as the law of nature. But in this complex world we as humans must care for 'Have Nots' also and accepting in society as well in our living system all these special need babies and humans as they are all part of our lives too at large. Sam, you have taught me that some time we panic for minor problems in our lives while there are others who are living happily and grateful to God for simply being alive and be able to breathe.

Sam, I know you have seen Georgie, a loving hustler which your auntie Dipika has got it and has visited us a few times. She is our grand dog and I know you like her and she likes to kiss your face and feet and you simply laugh with her and never feel upset when she jumps on your bed and on your chair to lick you. She has also made a friend in our neighborhood and her name is Nalini and is also a hustler dog. Georgie and Nalini whenever they get together they both runs after each other so fast that we have to leave Georgie free of her lease and they both give us so much pleasure when they run around each other. Nalini will be sometime come looking for Georgie in our back yard and will sit in our back yard. One day she simply came running to me as I was working in my backyard. Our friends who owns her were shouting for her and looking for her saying" Nalini, Nalini come back and I shouted loudly" That she is with me and don't worry, I patted her and she went back. If I go for a walk on her street she will come running to me for a pat. Sam likes listening to Georgie and Nalin's stories and laughs at them. Actually he wanted to hear my voice too relating to such stories. Sam, I know you had your soccer game today and also you had your Botox injections for your mobility. You are wonderful and feel proud of you for showing up on all these events you get involved. You are a very strong person physically and spiritually. I wonder how you manage all this, perhaps with the help of your mom. We all know she is very much dedicated to you and you are her life and she will never abandon you under ANY CONDITIONS. We all feel same way about you and all your family is behind your welfare and health.

SAM, sometime I wonder why people object helping human beings like you for their own beliefs which may or may not be really correct. I feel all of us should give a second look of whatever we believe in. Life is bigger than even our own beliefs and life changing every moment and we should be adjusting our thinking, beliefs and thoughts almost every day to really understand the purpose of our existence and from where and how we happened to come to this planet and for what reason.

SAM, I was kind of a little eccentric from very beginning. I was sleeping when all my classmates and friends were awake and I was up and studying and doing homework given by teachers when everyone else in my dorms were sleeping. Ryan you are almost like me as you do everything whenever you want except your motor skills to do whatever you want to do with your muscles, arms and legs. I know you love to talk but you cannot because of your throat muscles fail to listen to your brain message to speak. We all still understand your feelings AND YOUR ACTIONS and your zesters to explain what you want. You are a brave boy and always fought to survive exactly like your nana. I think life is mostly a war of survival and also a war of being to understand why and how we came into existence and who controls all that. All our ideology and beliefs should circulate around that and not on our beliefs which were created simply because of our growing up in certain environment and certain area of world which over powered our own thinking by sticking to norms of that time of society. I always felt life is always more than that and is beyond our prejudices and belief systems if really believe in any prophet or god. God did not create us to kill each other with hatred and any different of opinions.

SAM, now I want to tell you how we all happened to be the citizen of UNITED STATES OF AMERICA. You are very fortunate that you are a born US citizen by law but most of our family, your mom, your auntie Dipika had to struggle to be the citizens of United States. Your uncle Surej is almost like you and he was born in United States and both of you are our own leaders who have guided us about many things and that is why we love both of you a lot. Your mom and your auntie Dipika had to go to court in Cleveland, Ohio along with your Nanni, to get naturalization and citizenship. SAM, you are born in this country and you are ahead of all of us and you should feel great simply where you were born and our whole family loves that you are a born citizen of USA and all of us had to struggle to get the citizenship which you were born with this constitutional rights. SAM, you are a wonderful person in our family and we all know that everyone in our family will not only love you but you will be an inspiration to all of the family. You inspire us all simply by telling us all that our problems are trivial as compared to most problems in the world.

SAM, you had some rights in this country we all call our home because you are born in this country. You and your uncle Surej and your younger brother Griffin are the only three family members who are the USA born citizens and all other are naturalized citizens. Same way on my brother side of the family, your uncle Anil, Deepak and your cousins Nate, John, Liz, pat, and Bob are all born citizens in USA citizens and rest of them are also naturalized citizens except your uncle Charles.

As I came to USA in 1971 March and I took citizenship by naturalization laws and sometime in 1976 approximately which was roughly after five years of my immigration to USA. But that is not as important as naturalization of your mom, auntie Dipika and your Nanni. They were all naturalized in August of 1981 in US District Court of the Northern District of Ohio in Cleveland, Ohio. Your mom was twelve year old and your auntie Dipika was ten year old. As they were both minors, under the naturalization laws they were supposed to get automatically citizenship after their mom get citizenship. At that time I was already a citizen. Your Nanny got a letter from the judge who was presiding her naturalization ceremony that he would like to choose her for a speaker from a group of about 120 immigrants and she would be speaking on the topic" Why you chose to be a citizen of USA". Your Nanni replied by letter and agreed to give a speech in the court.

I was surprised that she agreed and she started thinking and started taking help from her own resources mostly friends to prepare for the speech. I only remember standing in the doorway of a hall with your uncle Surej and your Nanni,your mom and auntie Dipika were all sitting in the front chairs in the hall and all other "Soon to become citizens "were sitting in the front also on chairs. I was standing and waiting to listen to what your Nanni would say in her speech. I finally managed to get the one page speech which I attached on the next page. Her speech which appeared in newspapers of Toledo, Cleveland and other papers of our locality at that time.

Why I Chose to be
An American Citizen
(By Baljit)

I consider it a very, high honor to have the opportunity to speak, for this group of new citizen of the United States of America. All of us cherish this new citizenship very much.

I came to the United States ten (10) years ago to be with my husband, who had come over here about a year earlier. He is employed as an electrical engineer. We separated ourselves from the strong ties of family and friends to come to this country, where a great economic and social opportunities exist. These opportunities make it possible for us to improve the quality of 1ife for ourselves and our children. We are happy to choose the quality of life we want, and then work to attain that level of living.

Our children can be raised, in a wholesome atmosphere almost-entirely void of disease and hunger. They can attend schools, where they can learn skills which will enable them, to enter the Job market, on at least a semi-skilled basis.

We treasure the right we have to vote on who will represent us in government, and to freely express our views on any and all issues and subjects. It is a little disturbing, to find so many to avail themselves of this right of citizenship.

A few days ago our family spent a day at Kings Island Amusement Park near Cincinnati. I mention it here, because it is an example of the many opportunities we have in this country, for families to enjoy things together.

Why do I want to be a citizen of the United States? I want to join the millions who have come to this country, searching a new and better way of life. I hope to join all of these, before me.in making the United States of America truly the Melting Pot of hope for all peoples of the world.

I accept citizenship with great feelings of hope and with the promise to fulfill the duties of citizenship.

Thank you,

Signed by

Baljit

Sam! You are a unique being, made from same atoms and the same energy as the rest of us and the universe. We understand you do have specific DNA Thus, at the heart of this Universe made of magnetism and vibrations you emit and receive vibes. Remember you and all other like you are part of the Great Wholeness. My beloved grandson, remember "Life is just a journey in a train which always you like riding and which you only select where STOP and get down or board without having any control over start and ending of your train route and overall journey. We should simply be highly grateful for the train ride or the life existence which goes on and on and we should pay attention to STOPS, Board and Un board which are nothing but our own" Karma's or our own actions which can be positive or negative and can transform into exciting or depressive. Thinking as Negative will bring negative in your future existence AND IF YOU STAY AND THINK POSITIVE YOU WOULD BE HELPED BY AN EXTERNAL AND SPIRITUAL POWER AND CAN BE EXCITING OR IMPRESSIVE for your whole life time.

INTRODUCTION OF CHARACTERS IN THE STORY" A Journey of an IMMIGRANT and his first GRAND CHILD SAM" are as below:

SAM- A special need baby who has grown to be an young boy of eighteen year old and supposed to graduate from high school in next couple of years as a special need student and who has provided immense happiness to the family.

TONY- He is the younger brother of SAM who always was very bright in everything he does. He is a good soccer player in high school and is an + A student all over and has never given the family any problem.

KOMAL-

- SAM's mom who has dedicated her life for making him grow and never complained about any of her own problems in marriage life.

DIPIKA- SAM's auntie who has seen him with all kinds of problems and has been a consulting attorney for her sister and a great well-wisher for SAM.

SUREJ– SAM's uncle who loves him very much and would even stand up against his (SAM's) own Dad for his and his sister's concerns.

Nanni- is KOMAL's mom and SAM's, moms, mom (Grandmother from mother's side).In the story she has been mentioned as BALJIT, DOLLY or.

Nanna- is SAM's grandpa and SAM is his daughter's son and his first Grand Child who ended up to be a special need baby even after born as a normal child but suffered from an SID episode at the age of about three months while being with a baby sister the first time he was ever left for someone else to take care of him. SAM always responds to all kind of zesters and talks with Nanna. Nanna always loved his expressions which are always so real and we both love to be in each other's company all the time.

Urmi- is SAM's Nanni #2 and is Nanna's sister in law ie Nanna's brother's wife and has a close connect with family and all children and also is a great and long friend of Nanni.

John, Nate, Liz, Pat, Bob and Danny- are Sam's and Tony's cousins.

Sue and Josh Scott, Manu and Rick, Theni and Dr. Gupta, are SAM's uncle and aunties along with SAM,s uncle Anilk and Deep and his wife Asha

HARDEV and ARKEY- mentioned in the story are Nanna's long term friends of more than forty years and Nanna regards them immensely.

Printed in the United States
By Bookmasters